STRONGER THAN DEATH

By the same author

Thou Art There Also

Stronger than Death

Michael Paternoster

LONDON

S·P·C·K

1972

First published in 1972
by S.P.C.K.
Holy Trinity Church
Marylebone Road
London NW1 4DU

Printed in Great Britain by
Talbot Press (S.P.C.K.)
Saffron Walden, Essex

SBN 281 02657 2

In Memory of my Father

1907–1967

. . . . that body which was once a Temple of the Holy Ghost, and is now become a small quantity of Christian dust. But I shall see it re-animated.

Isaak Walton, *Life of Dr John Donne*

CONTENTS

Acknowledgements		viii
Author's Note		ix
1	The Last Enemy	1
2	Stronger than Death	15
3	He is Risen	28
4	. . . We are Risen	48
Notes		70
Index		75

ACKNOWLEDGEMENTS

Thanks are due to the following for permission to quote from copyright sources :

Hamish Hamilton Ltd : *Collected Poems*, by Kathleen Raine.

Hodder & Stoughton Ltd : *Sword at Sunset*, by Rosemary Sutcliffe.

John Murray (Publishers) Ltd : *Collected Poems*, by John Betjeman.

SCM Press Ltd : *The Shaking of the Foundations*, by Paul Tillich; *The Glory of Man*, by David Jenkins.

The Editor of *Theology* and the Reverend Paul Oestreicher: a quotation from an article entitled "Christians and Communists in search of Man" in *Theology*, vol. LXX, no. 570 (December 1967).

AUTHOR'S NOTE

This book has taken nearly three years to write; it may seem a small thing to come from so much labour, but any merits that it may possess owe more to others than to me — first and foremost to my father, from whose life of unobtrusive witness sustained by regular Communion I have derived those insights I hope I have made my own; then to the Very Reverend Dr Alastair Haggart,* Provost of St Paul's Cathedral, Dundee, on whose staff I served for nearly five years, who twice read my manuscript and made many pertinent and illuminating comments; next to the Venerable Michael Perry, Archdeacon of Durham, who while on the staff of S.P.C.K. took untold trouble on my behalf.

* Now Principal of Edinburgh Theological College.

THE LAST ENEMY

O eloquent, just and mighty death! Whom none could advise, thou hast persuaded; what none hath dared, thou hast done; and whom all the world hath flattered, thou only hast cast out of the world and despised. Thou hast drawn together all the far-stretched greatness, all the pride, cruelty, and ambition of men, and covered it all over with these two narrow words, *Hic Jacet*.

Sir Walter Raleigh.

The thesis of this book can be briefly stated. Death is one of the facts of life, and it has to be faced. It is the symptom of something terribly wrong with the human condition; it is also a step on the way to putting it right. If death were the last word, human life would end in futility; but it is not the last word because God himself submitted to death and rose triumphantly from it. We have evidence of this, which falls short of demonstrable proof, but is weighty enough to be taken seriously; and if we do take it seriously, our lives, here and now, can take on a new quality which can give us some idea of what victory over death might mean for us.

Having stated the theme, there are two things to be said before going further. If any reader feels that this is going to bear too close a resemblance to my first book, *Thou Art There Also*, and is tempted to give it up, I hope he will persevere as, in my own mind at least, this is a different, though related enterprise. In a sense, I am beginning where I left off, and presupposing the truth of what I have argued before; in another sense, I am starting from the same place, death, and making for the same destination, God, but travelling by a quite different route. The argument before was mainly historical, and aimed at clearing away some misconceptions about the after-life. It was mainly concerned with the ideas of hell and purgatory, and much less with the idea of heaven. This time, hell and purgatory hardly come into the picture, and it is heaven and its earthly foreshadowings with which we shall be more concerned. Also, the arrangement of material is not in an historical, but in what I hope is a logical, sequence. This brings me to the second preliminary point, which will take a little longer to deal with.

I remember in my school-days having an argument with a friend about religion. He maintained that the Churches, if they wanted to make converts nowadays, would have to give up all this nonsense about "original sin", for nobody would be attracted to join a body which insisted that he must, to start with, admit that he was a miserable sinner. I argued that "original sin" was just one of the facts of experience, and the Church at least offered an explanation for it, and an escape from it, which ought to attract anybody aware of his real situation. I still hold this conviction, and the arrangement of this book depends on its soundness; but it is by no means self-evident that mine is the right approach. Before I am able to use it, I have to justify my choice.

In the past, Christian preachers and writers took it for granted that the proper course was to begin by telling, or reminding, potential adherents of their desperate plight, and then, having thoroughly alarmed them, to hold out the one guaranteed means of deliverance. The leaders of great religious revivals, such as Jonathan Edwards in America and John Wesley in Britain, deliberately and explicitly used this technique. Nowadays its validity has been questioned. In the precise form in which they used it it will, of course, no longer work; for it depended frankly on hell-fire. But is it still legitimate, or even possible, to bring men and women to God by first pointing out to them the horrors of life without God? You cannot produce love by playing on fear; and the Christian apologist cannot help noticing how the revivalist technique has been taken up and refined by psychiatrists and secret police for entirely secular ends. Again, we are dealing, in Western society at any rate, with a type of man to whom the gospel often cannot be meaningfully preached because he is quite unaware of, or unconcerned about, ultimate questions which need God for an answer. F.D. Maurice was worried about this possibility over a century ago; and now it is, apparently, a reality. Some theologians, notably Bonhoeffer, argue that the whole idea of "ultimate questions which need God for an answer" is an erroneous one, and that to entertain it is likely to prove disastrous for Christianity, as it confines God to the rapidly dwindling area where man cannot manage at all satisfactorily on his own. The time may come, perhaps has come, when that area vanishes altogether, and then where is God? Bonhoeffer remarks scathingly on the way that existentialist philosophers and psychotherapists

2

"demonstrate to secure, contented, and happy mankind that it is really unhappy and desperate and simply unwilling to admit that it is in a predicament about which it knows nothing, and from which only they can rescue it," 1 and maintains that any Christian apologetic that tries the same method is an attack on the adulthood of the world, and is "pointless, ignoble and unchristian".

Bonhoeffer's contention contains an important element of truth. It is clearly disastrous to relegate God to the unexplained gaps in human knowledge; Laplace was obviously right in his celebrated rejection of the hypothesis of God to explain certain scientific facts which could be satisfactorily accounted for without direct reference to him. But surely one cannot be so bemused by the spectacle of human knowledge gradually conquering more and more territory as to imagine that man can ever "do without God" in the only sense that really matters. God as an hypothesis to cloak our ignorance of causation within the closed circle of the universe is no longer necessary; but man, with all his knowledge, is still "a stranger and afraid, in a world he never made", as a leading humanist, Lady Wootton, admits in the title of her latest book. It is not man the scientist who needs God, so much as man the sinner: the man who finds his best efforts missing the mark; the man whose skill and goodness lead to Hiroshima.

More realistic than Bonhoeffer's dismissal of ultimate questions, or their evasion by the affluent, is the attitude of the Marxist philosopher, Roger Garaudy:

> Christianity raises questions which, even if they are wrapped in mystery, require answers. There are areas which Christianity has explored, where the fruit of experience could be enriching for Marxist thought. Take for example the problem of death. I am invited to a colloqium with the Dominicans on this question, and I arrive with empty hands. . . . In short, I think that all the answers which religion gives are out of date, and I think that some of its questions have been wrapped up in mystification, but I believe that the human experience which underlies these questions cannot be ignored by any doctrine, including Marxism. 2

The contention that it is wrong to begin by dwelling on the human predicament and trying to bring it home to people is supported sometimes by the plea that Jesus himself did not attempt to arouse a sense of guilt. J.B. Phillips, in *Making Men Whole*, insists on this, and comments: "I think we do ourselves and God a disservice by continually harping on our own sinfulness." 3 The context makes it clear that this is not just an example of English Pelagianism, but a conviction held in all sincerity *despite* a deep awareness of our imperfection and our need of God. But it rests on a false premiss. Even if it is true that Jesus did not use the preaching techniques of the revivalists, that does not mean that he minimized the fact of man's sinfulness and need of salvation. He could assume that an awareness of this already existed in the minds of his hearers. He was speaking, after all, to men who had the law and the prophets, and his way had been prepared by John the Baptist, who *did* use the revivalist technique.

It certainly looks as though the "good news" can have meaning only to those who have first heard "bad news". A century ago R.H. Benson wrote: "The bondage of Egypt must be felt ere the redemption could be accepted. Sin must be hated ere the Saviour could be loved. John came preaching repentance because the kingdom of heaven was at hand." 4 One of the most recent and delightful attempts to communicate Christian truth, *The Gospel According to Peanuts,* is of the same mind.

> In a sense, it is a "hard saying" or *bad* news to say that everyone must go "through a depression" in order to emerge in a new and infinitely more satisfying life. This is why the gospel, or "good news", is never *good* news except to those who are already "meek and lowly" or "of a humble and contrite Spirit"; this is why the gospel is always addressed to those "who have ears to hear" — those "who labour and are heavy laden". 5

It was, I believe, Niebuhr, who remarked that the cross was the revelation of the love of God only to those who had first stood under it as judgement.

I am, then, in good company if I continue to use the traditional approach of beginning with man's predicament and arguing from it for his need of divine intervention. Bonhoeffer wrote in a Nazi prison cell. I do not think that the realities of the world we live in can lead anyone to suppose that man is capable of achieving his own perfection. Further, even if all the horrors of war, disease, crime, and natural disaster were removed, there still remains the basic, inescapable fact of death, reminding us all of our own finitude. Were we all happy, healthy, and contented (which we are not) death would still come to ask us what is the point of it all. In a world of uncertainties death is one of the certainties. How or when it will come we never know, but come it will for all of us. The fact of death colours the whole of existence. It is not just the shears that cuts each thread; because we have memory, foresight, and imagination, it is itself one of the threads that make up the pattern. "Where, in youth, death was a macabre threat to other and older people, it suddenly becomes, in middle age, a definite entry on one's engagement pad." 6

And yet death nowadays is one of the topics we do not discuss. The Victorian taboo on sex has been replaced by a modern taboo on death. One can explain this partly by the fact that the conquest of disease has made death less familiar to members of our society; but yet, on the other side of the balance, the war memorials everywhere remind us of the ubiquity of violent death in the last fifty years. There are signs that the policy of repressing the subject of death has had results as disastrous in their way as those that followed from earlier forms of repression. Hence, members of the caring professions are becoming keenly interested in problems of death and bereavement; an editorial in a journal aimed at doctors, clergy, and social workers, remarked recently that issues on death now sell better than issues on sex. 7 Death, after all, does not go away if we try to dismiss it from our minds. What, then, are we to think about it? For it has a disastrously paralysing effect on life to dwell on death without having a coherent attitude to it. This is one of the lessons of *Hamlet,* the only great tragedy which may be said to be about death. In other tragedies death is the frame of the picture; in *Hamlet* the hero is constantly thinking about what lies beyond the grave, and thus

The native hue of resolution

Is sicklied o'er with the pale cast of thought.

This is probably the real reason why death is nowadays banished, as far as possible, from the conscious mind: because there is no generally-agreed view of the world and of human destiny that will, as it were, make it "thinkable". But refusing to face facts never pays in the long run. If we are to look death in the face, we must, at least provisionally, make up our minds about it. There seem to be five possible reactions to death. The first is trying not to think about it, which we have already dismissed as futile. The second is fear, which is natural enough, and perhaps universal. C.V. Wedgwood, in a broadcast talk on "Personality in History", quoted the Corsican patriot, General Paoli, as saying:

5

It is impossible not to be afraid of death, and those who at the time of dying are not afraid are not thinking of death but of applause, or something else which keeps death out of their sight; so that all men are equally afraid of death when they see it; only some have a power of turning their sight away from it better than others. 8

One must, however, distinguish two different fears. One is the fear of *dying,* which can be painful, degrading, or otherwise up-setting. This fear is often mistaken. Doctor Johnson spent his lifetime in terror of dying, and yet died in peace and serenity. The other is the fear of *being dead,* and this is the fear of the unknown. This is what Hamlet was afraid of; this is the fear we must all feel, unless we can arm ourselves with a robust faith.

The third attitude to death is to rail against it, to refuse to accept it. This is the attitude exemplified in Dylan Thomas' bitter poem, "Go not gentle into that good night". But setting oneself against the inevitable is the way to hellish misery.

The fourth attitude is to take death for granted; to ask, in effect, what all the fuss is about. The attitude is shared by people of completely contrary beliefs. There are, on the one hand, those who believe in no form of survival, but point out that the cycle of life and death is part of the order of things, from which nothing is exempt. Insects and flowers flourish and die in a matter of days, or even hours; the life-span of the earth and of the solar system is infinitely longer, but their eventual death and disintegration is inevitable. Why should we expect exemption from the common lot? Let us go cheerfully when our time comes. We shall have had our day.

At the other extreme there are those for whom survival after death is unquestioned, and an existence not necessarily disem-bodied is something to look forward to. Socrates, as the poison began to work, vowed a cock to the God of healing as if life were a disease and death the cure.

Going beyond this matter-of-fact acceptance of death, for what-ever reason, is the attitude which positively welcomes it. This is presumably rare, or suicide would be commoner than it is; but it occurs not only in those afflicted with some kind of "death-wish" but also in reasonably balanced people who see a real and positive value in their present existence but a greater value in some future existence. St Paul is one example that springs to mind. Other Christians have seen death as an opportunity for one last final and irrevocable affirmation of God and as an act of Holy Communion which unites them for ever with the Lord they have glimpsed fitfully, and frequently failed to serve, while struggling with everyday life. In an interview on his seventieth birthday Sir Malcolm Sargent cheerfully proclaimed that he was greatly looking forward to death, simply because he had loved this life so much. "When I go into the next world, I shall not feel a stranger. As a child taken from the left breast cries only to find consolation in the right breast, so shall it be when we pass from life to death, *from life to life.*" This attitude, broadcast to millions, he maintained in the loneliness of a long and painful illness; on his deathbed he told the Archbishop of York, "I always had faith. Now I have knowledge." 9

No doubt at different times in our lives we shall all feel the force of each of these different attitudes to death. There is all the difference in the world between discussing an issue theoretically and facing it in actuality. But if we are not to be carried away by the ups and downs of our emotional temperature, we need a firm basis of considered and reasonable belief arrived at calmly when we were relatively detached.

Let me say at once that the Christian view of death is neither that it is the end of everything nor that in itself it is nothing but an escape from prison. Death, for the Christian, is the first term in a process, of which the second is resurrection. For death is something profoundly and horribly unnatural. It severs things that are meant to belong together. It separates, first of all, and most obviously, body and soul, two things which are both essential to the complete human personality. Knowing as we do what death does to the body, how can we be sure that the soul survives unscathed? Again, it separates men from each other. Though all must die, each must die alone. Even those who have become one flesh must be torn apart by death: the vows of marriage are taken "till death us do part". This, too, is profoundly unnatural and repugnant. Then, thirdly, there is the separation of man from God. This, for the Old Testament, was the real sting of death, and there is evidence that even Jesus felt this separation come home to him on the cross: "My God, my God, why hast thou forsaken me?"

If death is such a profoundly unnatural process, it suggests that something has gone desperately wrong with a world which is not merely one in which death *can* occur, but one in which it is a universal and inevitable occurrence. Thinking about death leads us unavoidably to consider the "fallenness" of the world we know. Death is not of course the only, nor even on the whole the greatest, evil in our experience. But it is a symptom of something seriously the matter, and it is always a mistake to treat symptoms without accurately diagnosing the disease. Looking at what are, from our point of view, the unsatisfactory features of the world we live in, there seem to be, basically, five possible explanations.

The first is the one favoured by atheists and agnostics, whether or not they are, strictly speaking, materialists. This is that everything has come about by chance, without purpose or design, and that therefore it is to be expected that some of the results should strike us as undesirable; our interests were not consulted. This is, on further reflection, not really an explanation at all. It just accepts the chaos of phenomena as given and makes the best of it. To leave the matter at that point may be unavoidable, but it is hardly satisfactory. The merit of this view is that it does not deny that, left to ourselves, this is about as far as we can get. Any attempt at a comprehensive explanation which is based solely on the facts accessible to us in the ordinary way is necessarily incomplete and lacking in authority. This is the defect of any historical theory which claims to read the purpose of history out of a scrutiny of the events known to us at the moment. This is just sheer presumption. We have no guarantee either that we possess all the relevant facts or that our minds are capable of grasping their significance.

All the same, the human mind finds it difficult to accept that there is *no* explanation for the state of things as we know it, but that everything has come about by the mindless interactions of sheer chance. The world, for all its faults, seems too highly organized for that. Any real explanation has somehow first to account for the basic goodness of most things and secondly to account for the undoubted fact that something drastic has gone wrong. The simplest way of dealing with both is by some form of dualism, and the second and third explanations come in this category.

The second is what I would term "personal dualism". In this the two opposing principles of good and evil are personified as supernatural beings fighting a war to the death. The most developed form of personal dualism is the old Persian religion associated with the prophet Zoroaster. That there is not only a benevolent God but a malevolent devil accounts for a great deal that is otherwise outrageous, but to make the two principles coequal and coeternal really will not do. The point is this, that evil is always parasitic. Evil is always something good gone wrong. Goodness therefore must logically precede evil; though, if things are left to themselves, there is no logical reason why, once they have started going wrong, they should not get steadily worse and worse. No one nowadays is likely to regard personal dualism as anything but a mythological explanation of certain observed phenomena; but to make the myth acceptable the devil must be a subordinate figure, as he is in orthodox Christianity.

Again, this view contributes an important point which our final and satisfactory explanation must allow for, and that is that unless the good power is continually intervening, once things have started going wrong, the process is irreversible, and the situation goes from bad to worse. Left alone, wounds become gangrenous and disease spreads.

The third view is that form of dualism which is not derived from a conflict of wills but from the existence of two *kinds* of being — what one might call the dualism of the elephant and the whale. That is to say, the two things are not necessarily hostile; they just have nothing in common. The two elements are given different names in different systems: God and the world, perhaps, or mind and matter. Much Eastern thinking is dualistic in this sense, and the more ascetic forms of Christianity are deeply tinged with it. Salvation is then a process of escaping somehow from entanglement in an alien and unwanted environment. It is on this view that death is welcomed as a release from prison. This kind of dualism also underlies two philosophical systems which have had immense influence. The more recent, but more completely dead, is Cartesianism. For Descartes mind and matter were two different kinds of substance which existed on parallel lines but never really met. This view is an illegitimate conclusion from the obvious fact that man is, or has, both soul and body. But the two cannot be separated without destroying the personality to which both are necessary. Man is an ensouled body, or an embodied soul. The horror of death is that it produces, instead of one being, a corpse and a ghost. Both philosophers and theologians now agree, if they agree on nothing else, that Cartesianism was a blind alley.

The other, and older, view is now enjoying a revival in some quarters. That is the Platonic view that the imperfections of the world we know are due to the fact that God is doing his best with intractable material. The Christian doctrine that God created all things from nothing ousted this view for a long time, but the difficulties to which this in turn gives rise have led to Platonism being seriously reconsidered. Whitehead has argued persuasively for such a view of God, and a number of theologians, amateur and professional, have taken him up. Whitehead's view is not open to the crude objection, "Where did the matter come from, if God didn't make it?" Even so, there is something unsatisfactory about it. A God who *needs* the world is a limited God, and a limited God is not really God, even if we believe (with Whitehead, and against Plato) that the present imperfections of the world are not permanent and inevitable, but stages on the way to a total perfection towards which God is striving, within certain self-imposed limitations. An element of dualism is almost inevitable in our thinking about this intractable problem, but the dualism cannot be ultimate if the cosmos is to make sense. That is, dualism must not be there, inevitably, from the very beginning, and it must be resolved by the end.

We are left then with two versions of the Christian doctrine of the fall. On the traditional view Adam and Eve were created perfect and sinless, to inhabit a perfect world; but through their own fault they forfeited their privileges and dragged the whole creation down in their ruin. "Original sin" does not mean that we are individually culpable, but that we are through no fault of our own born into a situation that has gone wrong, and that we in some way inherit a tendency to go wrong ourselves, thus perpetuating and perhaps accelerating the downward movement.

There are certain difficulties about this view. Quite apart from the question whether the fall "really happened", there is the grave psychological difficulty of imagining how a being in secure possession of all possible felicity, including open and unobstructed communion with its Creator, could wantonly of its own accord abandon all its advantages upon any inducement whatever. Milton, for instance, clearly believes that Adam and Eve were not merely innocent, in the sense that a child can be said to be innocent (and so capable of being misled), but were possessed of virtue and wisdom far exceeding the best achievements of any of their descendants. If one asks how such beings, supposing them to have existed, could possibly be led astray, the problem is shifted one stage back, by introducing the tempter, who is on the traditional view regarded as himself the ring-leader in a pre-cosmic fall. To account for the fall of man it is necessary to bring in a fallen angel; but how do we account for the fallen angel?

These difficulties are not met by simply abandoning the idea of the fall, but by expressing it in a different way. This has recently been done brilliantly by Professor John Hick, who claims to find an adumbration of an alternative theory as early in Christian theology as Irenaeus, who belongs to the second century A.D.

For Irenaeus, unlike Milton, Adam is to be regarded not as a superman who inexplicably gave way to temptation, but as a primitive, innocent in precisely the sense that a child is innocent. Such innocence must be left behind in the progress through experience to settled and unshakeable goodness. In the Easter Proclamation at the midnight service of Holy Saturday occurs the audacious phrase, *O felix culpa!* "O happy fault, that merited such and so great a Redeemer." The Irenaean view of the fall may be described as a theology of the *felix culpa*. With all that misery that it has brought in its train, the fall had to happen, and we should be happy that it happened; for it has opened to us undreamt-of possibilities of communion with God through our risen Lord. Essential to this interpretation is that responsibility rests fairly and squarely with God. The conventional view of the fall is concerned at all costs to avoid blaming God for what happened; but God himself is not concerned to evade responsibility. Indeed, the incarnation and crucifixion can be regarded as his acceptance of responsibility. Why God chose to make a world such that a "fall" was bound to happen is another matter. Part of the answer is that what God is concerned about is to elicit from men a free and loving response, and this is clearly unreal or impossible unless they are faced with a genuine choice. Had we been created already perfect, and set in the immediate presence of God, we could not but have served him. Turning away would have been unthinkable. God had to set us at what Hick calls a "psychological distance" from himself, so that we had to seek for him, and make a real act of commitment and response.

One merit of this view is that it does not suppose that "the fall" happened as a distinct historical event, before which men existed in a state of unimaginable perfection. The Miltonic view is not really amenable to demythologization; it is either factually true or false. But a fall conceived as an inevitable loss of childish innocence in the infancy of the human race will fit in quite happily with the modern picture of man's gradual evolution from pre-human and pre-rational creatures.

Such a view will also be found to take up and answer the various points made by the theories we have discussed and dis-

11

carded on the way. It has in common with the other view of the fall the insistence that "original sin", a misleading term, has nothing to do with individual guilt, but has to do with an environment into which we cannot help being born and a character we cannot help inheriting, both of which are in some respects highly unsatisfactory. It has the advantage over that view, and also over what I have called "personal dualism", that it does not require some sort of cosmic personification of evil to account for what has gone wrong with a situation initially satisfactory. And, of course, it avoids any irreducible element of dualism by making God ultimately responsible, and at the same time it accounts for what is plausible and attractive in Whitehead's thesis by arguing that God has freely and deliberately designed a world in which his purposes are only gradually achieved, and achieved only with our willing co-operation. This accounts for our observing at any particular moment unfulfilled intentions and unresolved tensions. Finally, it takes up the insight that the world is not self-explanatory. It is part of God's intention that he should be to some extent concealed behind conflicting phenomena. Had he made the meaning obvious on the surface, the enterprise of eliciting a free response would have been frustrated; as it is, belief in God and in his goodness and loving-kindness is an act of faith, one option amongst several almost equally plausible.

All forms of Christianity have an answer to the objection that the universe is by itself inexplicable, since they insist that God can only be known if he chooses to make himself known. The evidence that makes men agnostics is what Christians would expect. But the Irenaean view perhaps comes nearest to offering a plausible explanation of this divine inscrutability; it is not arbitrary, but part of his whole plan and purpose.

If evil is parasitic upon a creation originally good, then, as we have suggested, it is possible to imagine an irreversible process of corruption. A cheese that has begun to go bad can only get steadily worse. Christianity accepts that this is so, but postulates a divine intervention to redress the balance. On the traditional view the life and work of Christ is no more than this; it is simply a rescue operation, to reverse the effects of Adam's fall, and would not have been necessary had Adam not sinned. On the Irenaean view the coming of Christ has a place in God's plan from the first; for it marks an immense step forward in man's relations with God, just as the "fall" is the necessary pre-condition for the kind of free response God wants from man.

12

There is, of course, a danger in taking this view of the fall and its consequences. We may come to regard all this undoubted evil with insufficient seriousness, simply because we take it as a deliberate and calculated risk on God's part. But if we do, we are either treating the unimaginable immensity of human misery with inexcusable levity or else picturing God as a monster. As Anselm reminded us in *Cur Deus Homo,* we must never underestimate the gravity of sin, or the cost to God in setting it right. As we shall see, the cross is God's acceptance of complete responsibility, and necessarily involves a theology of the pain of God. Having said this, it must also be insisted that this world is not exclusively a "vale of tears". To say that is to suggest that the Creator has done his work badly, as well as being a denial of the good in our experience, which is an element every bit as valid as the evil. If evil is essentially parasitic, then this is a basically good world, distorted mainly by human unwillingness to acknowledge the lordship of God. "Original sin" is a misleading term for the results of this refusal. It might be better to speak of "total depravity", provided that we make clear what is meant by the term. It is in fact an extremely useful way of describing a phenomenon we are forced, however reluctantly, to acknowledge as an inescapable feature of human existence. It does *not* mean that all men are equally and hopelessly evil in the eyes of God, that we are all hardened criminals without a trace of kindly instincts. Such a view is manifestly absurd, and its rejection probably lies behind J.B. Phillips' remark, quoted earlier, that we do God a disservice by harping on our own sinfulness. What total depravity *does* mean is that there is nothing in human nature that is exempt from corruption and the distorting effects of heredity and environment — not that man is totally depraved, but that he is depraved in his totality. Scholastic theology sometimes made the mistake of assuming that reason could operate soundly and validly, quite unaffected by the manifestly disordered state of our wills and emotions. Marx and Freud have scotched that idea: in a world of ideology and rationalization we realize that our thinking is not as rational as we would like it to be. There are, in fact, no infallibilities. Again, Victorian poets and novelists sometimes suggested that human love could be altogether pure and disinterested; we shall see later that this is a mere sentimentality. Nothing we do and nothing we are is exempt from this inevitable distortion. An outstanding symbol of this is provided by Hiroshima. Belsen and Auschwitz were diabolical, but lack the ultimate irony of the first atom bomb, a horror

13

released on the world as the result of conscientious decisions by men of at least average goodness who intended thereby to avert an apparently greater evil.

This, then, is the human condition as we know it. Unless God really is ultimately responsible and has the answer, it is a hopeless plight. The answer cannot possibly be expressed solely and entirely in this-worldly terms. The fact of death must be faced. Death as transition is presumably inevitable, since nothing and no one in this world is naturally immortal. But death as we experience it, with the fear that precedes it, the agony that accompanies it, and the desolation that follows it, is a bitter aggravation of an already imperfect lot. Unless some shape can be given to the unknown beyond, and some assurance given that death can be transcended and overcome, then it remains the ultimate futility, mocking all our efforts.

> The boast of heraldry, the pomp of pow'r,
> And all that beauty, all that wealth, e'er gave,
> Await alike th'inevitable hour.
> The paths of glory lead but to the grave.

Gray's Elegy

STRONGER THAN DEATH?

> Guess who now holds thee — "Death", I said, but there
> The silver answer rang: "Not death but love."
>
> Elizabeth Barrett Browning, *Sonnets from the Portuguese*

Prince Siddhartha Gautama, confronted by the "Three messengers" — a sick man, an old man, and a corpse — who brought home to him the human predicament, set out on the quest for enlightenment. In due course as the Buddha, the fully enlightened one, he proclaimed his gospel, in the form of the Four Noble Truths: all is suffering; suffering is caused by desire; the way to extinguish suffering is to extinguish desire; the way to extinguish desire is to follow the eightfold path. A Western Christian commentator notes that in the First Noble Truth,

> The Buddha taught that human life is marked by the characters of imperfection, impermanence, emptiness, lack of abiding reality and permanent value. Sometimes this first truth is summarised in the words "all is suffering", as if to suggest that there is nothing but suffering: it would be truer to say that in everything there is the element of suffering. [1]

So interpreted this is but another way of expressing the idea of "total depravity", which is not a theological dogma to be accepted in the teeth of experience, but a conviction arising out of experience. Since the experience is common to all men, it is not surprising to find it expressed and explained in a variety of ways. Novelists and poets have often done so more tellingly and hauntingly than the theologians, because they deal not with abstract ideas but with concrete situations. To cite just two examples, one remembers in Tolstoy's *War and Peace* the paralysing awareness that came to Peter Besukhov of "the omnipresent lie which tainted every task he undertook", [2] and Kathleen Raine's cry

> Forgiven and made pure, what of all this
> Self could remain?
> This person formed
> For sin, by sin?

> How could these hands be mine,
> Shaped as they are by all the ill I have done,
> Life of creatures taken,
> Blows given, delicate things broken,
> Struck violently, green textures torn,
> Another living being touched ungently—
> Shaped as they are by all life's restless cruelty,
> Forgiven, these hands must die. 3

Writers of sensitivity and insight are acutely aware of living in a fallen world, a world in which our best efforts go astray, and all of us are at one and the same time culpable, involved in a common guilt, and helpless, the victims of circumstance. It is not a cheerful picture, but it is only shocking because people had forgotten or denied the Fall and replaced it by a myth of progress and perfectibility — a myth which the events of the last fifty years have effectively exploded.

Even so, many people object that modern literature, with its obsession with the sordid and the disreputable in human nature, is not true to life. Things, surely, are not really as bad as all that. The objection is, up to a point, a valid one. Miss Valerie Pitt, in *The Writer and the Modern World* complains that if there is one thing present-day writers cannot express it is joy; and a true-to-life picture of the world we know must, of course, represent its joys as well as its griefs. Going deeper, she perceives a failure to produce a true catharsis. These writers give us no feeling of liberation or purgation; they remind us of the limitations of the human condition and of our own inextricable involvement, in such a way that we are oppressed and driven to despair. This means, among other things, that the writers of the twentieth century have not, so far, touched the heights of *King Lear* or the *Oedipus Rex*. It also means, as I remarked in *Thou Art There Also,* that they are better at depicting hell than in imagining redemption. Many indeed seem to deny that redemption is possible.

People may object to this "hell on earth" school on two grounds. One is a superficial refusal to probe the depths, and a preference for the comfortable, undisturbing fictions that make no demands and awake no terrors. This simply will not do, for all men, sooner or later, however cushioned, must come up against the hard edges of reality. If they do not do so before, they will do so when they die; and it is a terrible thing to fall unprepared into the hidden depths. This, then, is no real objection to what the writers are telling us; the true objection is that they do not go deep enough or far enough. They do not go beyond the vision of the pit to the hope of redemption; they do not see the temporal *sub specie eternitatis*.

But whether there is an eternal order at all is precisely the point at issue. Many today regard this as merely another piece of wishful thinking, to be exposed as such. The state of the world is taken by them as proof that God does not exist and does not care. One might instead argue that their very awareness of something wrong and indignation at it witness to the existence and reality of some transcendent standard of values; but its existence, clearly, must be argued and not assumed. Is it really possible to make out a case for a hopeful view of human destiny, in view of all we know about human depravity?

Valerie Pitt describes most modern literature as "a kind of macabre dialogue between Eros and Thanatos". 4 Eros and Thanatos — Love and Death — these are two key concepts, and everything depends on which is stronger. Can love conquer even death, or does death have the last word and doom all human experience to ultimate futility?

Death has already been defined in terms of separation — a three-fold separation of soul from body, of man from family and friends, and of man from God. If death really does destroy beyond recall the unity of the invididual personality and break all bonds between man and man, then nothing survives capable of communion with God. This, if true, is a severe limitation on God's power, so severe that it makes it highly probable that any sense of God we may enjoy in this life is an illusion. Certainly, unless he can offer hope beyond death, he is not able to resolve the contradictions of existence. If death has the last word, love is only a short-term palliative of a meaningless existence, and religion is not even that, it is mere fantasy.

What, then, is love, and how shall we define it? At the very least it must mean treating other people as persons and not as things. Manipulating them for one's profit or pleasure, or even "for their own good", is treating them as less than human. Love is parodied by lust on the one side, and by bureaucracy on the other. That people deserve to be treated as people is one fundamental moral principle that the twentieth century understands — even though it fails conspicuously to act on it. The primacy of the personal is a starting-point Christian and humanist have in common.

But love is more than just practising the golden rule — "whatsoever ye would that men should do to you, do ye even so to them" (Matt. 7. 12. AV). This, no doubt, is *something*, but love is usually regarded as going beyond this. It involves, to use a fashionable but imprecise term, a certain degree of commitment. It goes beyond the prudential to the sacrificial.

Now there is no doubt that there is a fair amount of love, so defined, in the world. Not every human being, unhappily, knows what "love" means; but most have a fair idea, from experiencing others' love for them, and from trying to love others. This respect and commitment they try to put into practice, if not in all their personal relationships, then at any rate towards certain individuals — individuals, incidentally, who are generally "given", not chosen. Moralists, and not only Christian moralists at that, are inclined to urge that love ought to play a much larger part in our lives and in the affairs of the world than it does, and to argue that if it did human society would cease to exhibit those features which lead men to describe it as "fallen". If this is true, there must be some reasonable prospect that such a programme could be carried out; but there does not seem to be.

In the wedding service vows are taken only "till death us do part". Laurence Whistler commented, in *The Initials in the Heart*, a recollection of his own brief marriage to Jill Furse, who died young:

> Couples are made by the Church to face the ending of their time together before it has fully begun. Death kneels between them, the merest shadow admittedly, not dreadful with ridiculous grimaces and spider hands, but folding his bleak sticks somewhat apologetically on the sensuous cushions. And we accepted him and were nearer at that moment than ever again to the funeral only one of us could attend. 5

Kathleen Raine remarks bleakly,

> Love binds in vain
> Whom death must loose. 6

In James Elroy Flecker's *Hassan,* the two lovers, Rafi and Pervanah, prefer to die together rather than live in lifelong separation, yet when they are dead their ghosts forget each other.

The reality is worse even than that terrible nightmare. It would not be so bad to forget or be forgotten when dead if one could love perfectly while one lived. Even this is denied us, it seems. "Each man kills the thing he loves." 7 Oscar Wilde's insight is true, and it is true because in even our purest loves there is an element of hate.

Love is strong, but perverted it can be a demonic force; and even at its strongest it meets its match at last. As Graham Greene says, in *The Heart of the Matter*, "In human love there is never such a thing as victory: only a few minor tactical successes before the final defeat of death or indifference." 8

Is there any way out of the cage?

One possible exit is that recommended by Buddhism: since desire leads to suffering, extinguish desire. Some Christians, notably St Augustine, take a similar line. It is, however, no better than a counsel of despair. It means giving up all that we normally, and rightly, regard as best in human life because of the pain it can bring, and forming no deep attachments because of the risk of heartbreak.

Surely a much more authentically Christian answer sees the way out in a direction diametrically opposite to the Buddhist one. Traherne wrote:

> For giving me desire . . . be
> Thy Name for ever praised by me.

So far as I know, the first Christian thinker, apart from Dante, to elaborate a theology of romantic love was Vladimir Soloviev. His ideas are, however, strikingly paralleled in the six "supernatural thrillers" of Charles Williams. Soloviev insisted that "falling in love" was a positive good, the first step towards the transfiguration of the entire universe and the final victory of life over death. He believed that love makes no promises it cannot fulfil, but the tragedy is that most human beings are so rapidly and completely disillusioned that they tend to dismiss their romantic dreams as unattainable. He saw quite clearly, however, that because "true love can never be satisfied till it sees the beloved delivered from the threat of death and decay and reborn in perfect beauty", men and women cannot attain the perfection they ardently desire unaided, and therefore "Man needs the Saviour". 9

One can, I think, only reasonably believe that love is stronger than death if one brings God into the picture. Without him the alternatives are wishful thinking or despair. It is quite true that "God" can be a form of wishful thinking, but only if one replaces the living God by some kind of man-made idol, if one turns the loving Father into a sentimental grandfather or pictures heaven simply as a never-never-land where dreams come true. The God of the Christians is not a cosy and domestic deity; he is to be found beyond despair, and his love immerses him more deeply than we can imagine in the ambiguities and distortions of this world.

The only love that *can* overcome death is the love of God; not our love for him, but his love for us. This must be so, for the obvious reason that only God is by nature immortal and so not of necessity subject to death; whereas we, whether we like it or not, must all submit to death, and without outside help are bound to perish utterly in the struggle.

When, however, we talk of the love of God, are we bound to redefine "love"? To some extent, yes; but not altogether, for if God's love were totally different from anything we had ever experienced in human love, it might well be all the same to us whether he loved or hated us. The love of God must be recognizable to us as love, or there is no point in talking about it. It must, then, involve the two elements we found in human love. It must at the very least be a matter of treating people as persons, and not things; and it must lead to a commitment.

If, in these terms, we say that God loves us, important consequences follow. It is inevitable that if he is to treat us as persons he must respect our freedom, which imposes limits on *his* freedom. This rules out a number of unworthy ideas about God. He is not free to impose his will on us by force; he must always persuade. This means not only that there is something sub-Christian and repellent in all pictures of an angry God endlessly tormenting any of his helpless creatures, however great their guilt, but also that there can be no *proof* of God's existence. The force of argument may be a more refined weapon than brute force, but it is equally coercive. Had we no choice but to believe in God, upon infallible proofs, we should have no freedom. We should not be human. The Irenaean doctrine of the Fall takes seriously the belief that God loves us enough to respect our freedom however we abuse it, and, more fundamental even than that, has placed us in a situation where we really do have freedom. Whitehead contrasts the view that God is "the supreme agent of compulsion" with another which he finds adumbrated in Plato, exemplified in Christ, and worked out in the theologians of the early Church — the view that "the divine element in the world is to be conceived as a persuasive agency and not as a coercive agency". 10 Or, in other words, "the limitation of God is his

20

goodness". 11 This suggests a way of answering the questions, sometimes captious, sometimes anguished, of people who ask, "Why does God allow evil?" To intervene decisively to stop any and every divergence from the path he intended us to take would not make God more loving towards us than he is; it would make him a tyrant. But to begin with, to have made a world in which evil was impossible and unthinkable would have been to make a race of robots, not of men, a race that could not be loved in the sense of being treated as persons.

But love, we have seen, involves more than this; it involves also a certain commitment. There can be no turning back, whatever the consequences. The bond is irrevocable: "for better for worse, for richer for poorer, in sickness and in health". If God's love is to be recognizable as love, it must possess this quality. The Bible assures us that it does:

> Can a woman forget her sucking child, that she should not have compassion on the son of her womb? Yea, they may forget, yet will I not forget thee. Behold, I have graven thee upon the palms of my hands (Isa. 49. 15-16, AV).

Religion, then, in its moments of deepest insight, insists that God will not give us up as a bad job. Whatever we do, however we abuse our freedom, we shall not exhaust his patience and tempt him to destroy us. In our Lord's parables, God is the father of the Prodigal who welcomes with open arms the son who has wasted the resources he lavished on him, even though the son is clearly culpable and can make no plea of diminished responsibility. (He is equally the father of the unloving and unlovable elder brother, whose attitude to life so many of us share.) He is also the shepherd, who seeks far and wide the lost sheep — a creature who may initially have strayed of its own accord but who is now so completely lost that it cannot find its own way back and can only wait, bleating, to be rescued. To picture us as prodigal sons or as lost sheep is not, perhaps, very flattering, and only excessive familiarity dulls the sense of shock we should otherwise feel; but these two images clearly represent two elements in the human predicament of which there can be no doubt: that we are all, to some degree, guilty of failing to live up to standards we unhesitatingly acknowledge as binding on us; and that we are all, at the same time, victims of heredity and environment, unable to escape from our predicament however hard we try. God knows all this, and in him absolute justice and

21

absolute mercy meet. There is a sense in which it is true to say that to understand everything is to forgive everything.

God, then, loves us as persons, and goes on loving us whatever we do, however unlovely we become. He respects us, and he is irrevocably committed. But there must be in his love a third element if we are not to picture him as simply a tribal deity; his love must be universal. He must treat every individual as a person; he must feel for each and every one that passionate self-giving concern that we ourselves can achieve only fitfully in one or two specially close relationships. Otherwise, his love does not really overcome the tensions and frustrations we feel so acutely, but merely adds to all life's other injustices the supreme injustice of favouritism on the part of the Creator.

It is perfectly clear, of course, that a great deal in the Bible, and in popular religion at all periods, can be used as evidence to suggest that the love of God does not measure up to these standards. Omnipotence is almost invariably pictured as an omnipotence of force, not of love; it is widely assumed that God's patience is fairly quickly exhausted; and the recipients of his favour are regarded as a privileged minority. It will be readily seen, however, that to fall short of ascribing to him love in the fullest sense is to involve oneself in contradiction. If his omnipotence is pictured in terms of power, then the problem of evil is totally insoluble: either God is not good, since he permits it, or he is not after all powerful enough to prevent it. Again, unless his love is undeviating and universal, it would seem that his character possesses flaws apparent even to such imperfect beings as ourselves. Whereas, if he is to be defined wholly and completely in terms of love (and this, after all, the New Testament asserts in so many words), then the apparent contradictions fall into place. They are all part of a risky, but intelligible, enterprise undertaken by God to bring about a situation in which his love is freely reciprocated. If this is true, or even plausible, the present state of affairs, bad as it is, leads not to despair, but to hope.

It is all very well to assert this, but, if it is to be more than mere assertion, one ought to be able to point to evidence of God's character. Here, of course, one is immediately confronted with a difficulty which, if this view is correct, is of his own devising: *nothing about God can be proved.* We have said that God has chosen not to force our assent by any means. An unkind critic might assert that we have merely elaborated a theory proof against any attempt at falsification. This is not, in fact, entirely

22

fair. The Christian hypothesis is, in the long run, verifiable; but it is a very long run indeed. John Hick, in an article, "Theology and Verification", which he first published in 1960, put forward the hypothesis of "Eschatological Verification", which he illustrated by a parable of two travellers on a road. One thinks it leads to the celestial city, the other thinks it leads nowhere.

> During the course of the journey, the issue between them is not an experimental one. They do not entertain different expectations about the coming details of the road, but only about its ultimate destination. Yet, when they turn the last corner, it will be apparent that one of them has been right all the time and the other wrong. Thus, although the issue between them has not been experimental, it has, nevertheless, been a real issue. 12

If those who see this life as hopeless and without meaning and who think of death as the ultimate futility are right, then they can never prove they are right. So long as life continues, the other alternative is a real option; and after death, on their view, there is no one left to say "I told you so". The Christian, however, can hope to prove his point in the next world, if not in this. This, of course, presupposes that some kind of victory over death is credible — which is precisely the point at issue. If we have to wait until we are dead to know whether anything can be done about our situation, there seems very little point in discussing it. Anything we decide to think or do is equally a shot in the dark. But the situation is not really as bad as that. God's omnipotent love is, for very good reasons, something we cannot yet prove; but it is something we can already experience. Commitment is called for on our part to begin with, but it is a commitment that is amply rewarded, even in this life.

Why, though, should we make this venture of commitment? Why should we put our trust in the love of God when we can never achieve demonstrable certainty about it in this life, and cannot even arrive at certitude until after we have taken the plunge? There is an answer, and it is that God has not left himself entirely without witness in this world. Many signs, looked at in the right way, point to him, and without him are pointless. More than anything else, there is the life of Jesus of Nazareth, in which Christians see the completest possible revelation of God, because in it we see, not yet another prophet sharing his insights with us, but God himself making himself known by living a human life. Of course such a self-revelation is also at the same time an incognito. In the nature of the case God could not *prove* that he was present to a unique degree in the life of Jesus without abandoning the very principle of non-coercive love; as John Donne put it, quaintly, but with an insight rare in his century: "Christ beats his Drum, but he does not Press men; Christ is served with Volunteers." 13 In any case it is hard to see just what would constitute unmistakable proof.

If the writers of the Gospels are right in the assertion, which they undoubtedly make, that Jesus was God incarnate, then all they tell us of him confirms that God's character can be defined in terms of absolute, unconditioned love. To make himself known by this means at all involves both a respect for human freedom and personality and an overwhelming yearning and concern for straying, sinful, suffering mankind — a respect implied by refusing to come in power and glory and compel belief, a concern implied by a willingness to go to such extreme lengths to set right the human situation. Jesus, we are told, at the outset of his ministry, met and resisted the temptations to compel belief, or to compromise with the world and enter into the moral ambiguities of government, or to put God to the test. Because he insisted on maintaining an integrity we may envy but cannot achieve, his failure, in worldly terms, was certain; and yet, of course, it was only by resisting the corrupting pressures that make us what we are that he could hope for any long-term success. Paradoxically, even in worldly terms he made the right choice. His contemporary, Augustus, felt bound, in order to achieve anything, to accept the moral ambiguities of human society; he was both murderer and victim, but he achieved a precarious peace. His achievement must not be minimized. Few men have done so much good; and he paid the price with his eyes open. Yet the stable society he hoped would last for ever — how short a time before it collapsed! Whereas Jesus dying on the cross did indeed, as he predicted, draw men to him. His is the attraction of an unattainable ideal made actual. But Christians wish to assert more than that Christ has exerted an appreciably greater influence on history by dying in apparent failure than he would have done by establishing a temporal, and therefore temporary, empire, whether by force or compromise. This may well be true; but they wish to assert rather that the cross of Christ is the supreme revelation of God's unresting, unchanging, and ultimately invincible love. To them God can say in a sense unforeseen by the prophet, "I have graven thee upon the palms of my hands." If true, this is an awe-inspiring thought.

For it to be true one must be able to say two things: that God was in Christ, and that the cross really was a victory. To take the latter first, it must be possible to give some meaning to the phrase, "the finished work of Christ". *Something* must be achieved by the cross that can be described as the defeat of sin and death, and that can be regarded as the start of a now irreversible process of putting right what has gone wrong — the start, only, because, if there is not also a sense in which we can refer to "the continuing work of Christ", then frankly nothing has been achieved that is worth calling a victory. If God has, as it were, shot his bolt, and done his utmost to put right the world's wrongs, then the fact that two thousand years later the most favourable and generous estimate cannot regard them as much improved means that God's love *has* been defeated. We can, however, choose to regard the cross as a decisive engagement with the forces of evil, one which guarantees ultimate victory. Then any evidence we can bring of Christ's continuing work will only reinforce our conviction that the cross was literally crucial — the turning-point in the whole campaign.

To define more precisely than this what exactly Christ's death achieved, or how it achieved it, is to run into endless difficulties. In particular, it is an unfortunate feature of a number of atonement theories of the past that they implicitly deny the other essential proposition — that God was in Christ. To say, as some have done, that Jesus is the lightning-conductor which averts from us the wrath of God is in fact to make nonsense of the whole procedure. It sets up an opposition between the Father and the Son, and it supposses that God's intention towards us was not always one of love. And yet attempts to explain the atonement along these lines have at times been so widely accepted among Christians as to make any other explanation almost unthinkable. Certainly, when a century ago F.D. Maurice attacked this kind of theorizing about the atonement as immoral even by the standards of unbelievers, he was rebuked by a Regius Professor of Divinity for impugning *the* "Doctrine of the Atonement", and for daring to imagine that the outsider had anything useful to say about the mysteries of the Christian faith. No longer now can we afford to ignore the attitude of sensitive and well-disposed agnostics; nor can we defend on the grounds of "mystery" man-made explanations of no great antiquity or authority which not only offend against the moral sense of mankind but also miss

25

some of the deeper insights of the New Testament. No doctrine of the atonement can approach the truth which ignores the key text: "God was in Christ, reconciling the world unto himself" (1 Cor. 5. 19, AV). Some would translate this as "In Christ, God was reconciling the world to himself". To do so *may* modify our view of the person of Christ, but it does not in the least diminish the involvement of God. For if we take this assertion as central, then we must say that when we look at the cross, we see God suffering. Orthodox Christians have always been reluctant to do this, partly on the excellent ground that there is a danger of confusing the persons of the Trinity, as in the Patripassian heresy. Christ is not to be identified with the Father. One suspects, however, that the real motive for denying the suffering of God is the same as the motive we detected in the "orthodox" doctrine of the Fall — the desire not to attribute responsibility to God. But the whole point of the cross is that there God accepts responsibility. The Japanese theologian, Kazoh Kitamori, wrote in a book published soon after Hiroshima, "The heart of the gospel was revealed to me as the 'pain of God'." [14] David Jenkins is prepared to assert, "Unless God suffers, there is no God." [15] A God who allows suffering but remains utterly detached is a cosmic sadist. But surely a God who suffers is less than completely divine? Traditionally God is depicted as impassible, but Canon Jenkins sees this as meaning that

> God is in no way dependent on anything outside himself for being himself, and that further, and more importantly, nothing whatever can put him off being God. He is the Lord, and he does not change. . . . He has made it known to us that the energy which manifests the essence of his being, in so far as manifestation is possible, is the energy of love. His unchangeability, therefore, is unquenchable love which can and does suffer everything at a deeper level of fully personal experience than is either open to or endurable for any of us, but this makes not one iota of difference to the reality of his love. [16]

If such assertions as these are true, one might, indeed, point to the cross and say "God loves like that!" Many have done so, from the first disciples to the present day. But others, no less sincere and sensitive, can see in the cross only the most outstanding evidence that death is stronger than love. Few there are who would deny the goodness or attractiveness of Jesus, or that he did consistently live his life on the principle that love is the supreme value; but many would deny that events vindicated his belief. One remembers Schweitzer's haunting picture of Jesus putting his shoulder to the wheel of history to make it turn, and then being crushed by it when it did.

The truth is that one can only see in the cross the supreme revelation of God's love if one looks at it in the light of the resurrection. Those who deny the resurrection, whether agnostics or liberal Christians, have to admit that the vision of Jesus is something of a wistful dream which will not stand up to harsh reality. But the resurrection is evidence of victory over death. We cannot, then, either assert or deny that love is stronger than death until we have taken the resurrection into account.

HE IS RISEN . . . .

> It is not just that Jesus is alive. It is that the Messiah reigns, and that therefore heaven and earth tremble on the brink of re-creation. 1
>
> Neville Clark

There is no doubt at all that the death of Christ really happened. The great question is whether the resurrection really happened. This is a question which Christians themselves are seriously discussing nowadays, to an extent that has not occurred for centuries. There is a widespread feeling that the old *Habeas Corpus* or detective story approach is simply not good enough any more. We have all heard Easter sermons which set out, and demolish, all the rival theories, on the assumption that the Gospels are eye-witness accounts to be taken literally, and that this is an event like any other event. The most thorough, extended, and in its way convincing example of this approach is Frank Morison's *Who Moved the Stone?* The defects of such attempts to "prove" the resurrection beyond a shadow of doubt are threefold. First, there is too great a readiness, generally, to accept the New Testament evidence at its face value, finding ingenious, plausible, and matter-of-fact explanations for its discrepancies. Secondly, the fundamental question of what we mean by "resurrection" is not answered, because it is not even asked. It is assumed that we all know what would count as a resurrection; but in fact the matter is not as straightforward as that. Then, thirdly, the most glaring defect of the detective-story approach is that it concentrates attention entirely on what did or did not happen a long time ago, on the first Easter day, whereas the gospel, if it is to be a gospel, *must* be about the present. The message is not simply, "Jesus was raised from the dead", but "Jesus *lives*". Its authentication does not, then, depend primarily on our ability to show we know what really happened on one particular day in history, but on any evidence there may be that people directly encounter Jesus now. There is, of course, an inevitable circularity about this argument, as put forward by committed Christians; they believe that God raised Jesus from the dead because they believe he is alive now, and they believe he is alive now because they believe

God raised him from the dead. Despite the circularity the two propositions support, rather than undermine, each other. Clearly, the past event would be of no significance whatever did it not lead to a real and definite change in the present situation; but the believer cannot jettison the past event as of no interest to him simply on the ground of the overwhelming certitude he enjoys in the present. His chances of contact with Christ, and through Christ with God, depend on something having happened to reverse the apparent tragedy and failure of Good Friday.

Jesus really died a slow painful death on the cross, was really buried, and went where all the dead go — wherever that may be. So much is unquestionable fact. The theory that he only fainted on the cross and revived in the cool of the rock-hewn tomb, though it is still put forward in the Sunday papers from time to time, is almost too absurd even to refute. It presupposes on the part of Jesus' executioners a degree of careless incompetence unlikely in any circumstances and doubly unlikely in a case which might have had serious political repercussions; to say nothing of attributing to Jesus, weakened and wounded as he certainly was, recuperative powers compared with which a direct intervention by Almighty God might well seem the lesser miracle. This theory, and others like it — such as that the women went to the wrong tomb, and nobody ever thought of checking up before wild rumours had already gone too far to be recalled — derive what little plausibility they possess from the rationalist dogma that this is a closed universe and miracles do not happen. Take that assumption for granted — and it cannot be proved — and it follows that once you have excluded the miraculous, whatever is left, however improbable, must be "what really happened".

There is, then, no satisfactory explanation in saying that the man Jesus did not really die. It is, however, unfortunately true that many Christian presentations of the resurrection, entirely orthodox in intention, implicitly deny that his death was real. Because he was God, as well as man, it was somehow different for him. He knew it would all come out right in the end. God can't die, so Jesus on the cross only seemed to be dead. Certainly the Gospels maintain that Jesus predicted not only his death but his resurrection, and claimed to find the whole pattern foreshadowed in the Old Testament, and in the Fourth Gospel particularly Jesus seems very much a being from another world, secure and unshakable in his knowledge of the outcome, untouched by pain and doubt. But this is only one aspect of the portrait of

Jesus in the New Testament, and comes out most clearly in the account written longest after the event, an account which is constantly concerned to probe beneath the surface events to the eternal significance, apparent in them only after long pondering. Even in St John it would be untrue to say that he stresses exclusively the inhuman air of omniscience and assurance with which Jesus meets every crisis; rather, he is trying the almost impossible task of holding two things in tension — the triumph of the cross, and the ordeal it involved. He records two words from the cross that balance each other — "I thirst" and "It is accomplished". The earlier account, given by Mark and taken over with slight amendments and elaborations by Matthew, emphasizes the tragic loneliness of Christ's death, and records only one word from the cross: "My God, my God, why hast thou forsaken me?" Here, undoubtedly, the death of Christ is a real death, characterized from within by all those forms of separation we have seen to be involved in the process of dying. His personality was split into a corpse, buried in a tomb, and a ghost, sent to join all other ghosts in "hell"; and, as this physical disintegration approached, he felt deserted not only by all his friends but even by God. The starkness of Christ's death in the Gospels cannot be exaggerated, and yet Christians draw back from accepting the implications. Preachers on the Seven Words from the Cross will tell you that "My God, my God, why?" was a quotation from an appropriate psalm, and that "I thirst" was not a cry of torment but a request to have his lips moistened so that he could, in the next word, announce his triumph. This kind of exegesis imports an air of unreality into the whole proceeding, and undermines its significance for us. Christ is no help to us either as a saviour or as an example if his sacrifice was a charade, and if the happy ending was a foregone conclusion. I find myself in complete agreement with the reported words of Professor Garaudy: "Jesus did not know in advance that he had won. This was not a stage death, after which the hero arises and bows to the applause of the audience." 2 If one asks why people, whatever they believe in theory, find it so hard to accept seriously that Christ's death was human, complete, and tragic, I suspect that the explanation lies in that false reverence that is unwilling to involve God too deeply in our affairs. It is, in fact, the same motive which tries not to make God responsible for evil by blaming Adam or the devil, and tries to deny that God can in any sense be said to suffer. It is, however, just as well for the human race that God does not share the views of some of his well-wishers. He is prepared to accept responsibility, fully and unreservedly, for the world he has created, and to take the consequences — and the consequences include, for him as for us, real pain and real death.

There is this much truth, at least, in the "Death of God" school. God really did die. But he is not still dead, as they aver. What they do is to construct a mythology, according to which there was once a transcendent God, "up there"; but he entered his own world as a man, and was put to death, so now there is no God. Jesus enjoys a kind of immortality within history, but there is no after-life, and no other world than this. The only difference between a Christian and an atheist is that, while both agree there is no God now, the Christian asserts that there was one once. To state the thesis briefly is to expose its absurdity. It is an impossible attempt at compromise between religion and atheism. If there ever was a God such as the Judeo-Christian tradition proclaims, then there still is; for his name is "I am"; he is the one being whose existence is underived and upon whom all other beings depend entirely for their existence. If, on the other hand, the idea of such a self-existent being is now unnecessary or incredible, it never was true, however many millions once believed it. That, none the less, the "death of God" school has created a stir and collected a following suggests that its appeal is not primarily an intellectual one. It answers to a felt need to be thoroughly modern and secular and yet to give life a religious dimension of some kind. What its myth represents is the fact that the *idea* of a transcendent God was once relevant and helpful, but for many people today this is no longer the case. The theory is that if religion is to survive it must frankly recognize that "God" as a transcendent being is obsolete and that if he can be said to exist at all he is wholly immanent. Before committing ourselves to a policy of eradicating "God up there" from Christianity, we might look at Buddhism. The Buddha had no need of the hypothesis of God; he called on men to save themselves, and offered them the necessary insight into their condition. He was, as Jung acutely observed, not so much a metaphysician as an outstanding empirical psychologist. In fact, however, men are so far from being able to save themselves, that many of the Buddha's followers have deified him, thus admitting their need of a transcendent saviour. If God does not exist, man is not liberated from an intolerable burden; he is, rather, crushed by one.

Christianity safeguards both the reality of God's death and the

31

reality of his continuing existence by the doctrine that God, though personal, is more than a person; he is better described as a family. When God became man, he did not, to use mythological language, abdicate his throne in heaven, leaving the world to run itself for thirty-three years while he was wholly occupied in one small corner of it. And when he died, there was no weekend interregnum in the divine government of the world. Somehow we have to say that "God was in Christ reconciling the world to himself", but that at the same time God continued to be what he always had been. Christ was wholly God; but he did not contain the whole of God, leaving no remainder. We can say, then, that death is a fact in the experience of God, but we cannot say, without qualification, that God died. The Patripassian heresy was condemned because it implied just this; but not every doctrine of the pain of God is Patripassian, and to say that suffering and death are as real to God as they are to us is to say something demanded by the orthodox interpretation of Christ's life and death.

We can say that the cross demonstrates the extent to which God is willing to accept responsibility and take the consequences, by becoming involved, and the lengths to which he will take his choice of persuasion rather than force. In short the cross reveals the love of God; but we can say this only if we can be sure that the cross is really a divine victory and not just a human defeat. This means that we can only derive from the cross its Christian significance in the light of the resurrection. Again, if God wishes to convince us that death has been conquered and that there is a way of escape from futility and meaninglessness, then two things are equally necessary: a real encounter with death, and a real return from that encounter. We might say, the Messiah *had* to die in order to overcome death. The grave is the only place from which, convincingly, new hope could spring. One of Tillich's sermons begins:

In the Nuremburg war-crime trials a witness appeared who had lived for a time in a grave in a Jewish graveyard in Wilna, Poland. It was the only place he — and many others — could live, when in hiding after they had escaped the gas chamber. During this time he wrote poetry, and one of the poems was a description of a birth. In a grave near by a young woman gave birth to a boy. The eighty-year old gravedigger, wrapped in a linen shroud, assisted. When the new-born child uttered his first cry, the old man prayed: "Great God, hast Thou finally sent

32

the Messiah to us? For who else than the Messiah Himself can be born in a grave?" But after three days, the poet saw the child sucking his mother's tears because she had no milk for him. 3

The old gravedigger was disappointed, as men have been disappointed time and again. But once, and once only, new life was born in a grave; and that new life was endless and undying. A recent novel, *The Davidson Affair,* presents the story of the resurrection as it might have been covered for television, in the form of a series of interviews first with the authorities, and then with the disciples. For the first few people approached "God can't die" is axiomatic, and for that reason Jesus, who undoubtedly died, cannot be God. But then the interviewer meets Mary Magdalene.

"Death can't hold God".
Neither Nicodemus nor Thomas Didymus had dared to say that. "God can't die" was the brick wall beyond which they could not go. But "Death can't hold God" was the statement of a woman on the other side of that wall. A woman living in a new dimension, beyond the fear of death. That was the secret of her assurance: the absolute security upon which she stood serene. 4

Evidently, then, the resurrection is an essential part of the Christian faith and the Christian proclamation. As St Paul said, "If Christ be not risen, then is our preaching vain, and your faith is also vain" (1 Cor. 15.8, AV). The whole point is that there is an escape from the futility of an existence that ends inevitably with death. If that is not true, Jesus was simply deluded.

But is the resurrection believable? There is nothing specially modern about answering "No". The Athenians on the Areopagus greeted St Paul's insistence that God had raised Jesus from the dead with polite scepticism. We need not therefore be bemused into imagining that it is living in the twentieth century that puts insuperable difficulties in the way of our believing it. It is unthinkable only if one assumes from the outset that God cannot or will not intervene or that there is no God to intervene. George Bernard Shaw, in the preface to *Androcles and the Lion,* one of his most brilliant displays of misplaced ingenuity, professed to take the Gospels as they stood, not picking and choosing, and to see what he could make of them. Whether by sleight of hand or by sheer oversight, he did not even consider the resurrection. Perhaps he simply took it for granted that no one could take that seriously. Another Irishman, W.B. Yeats, though no more a Christian than Shaw, did take it seriously, and in his short play *The Resurrection* presented an unforgettable picture of the impact it must have had on the disciples who, whatever they were expecting, were not expecting *that*. Greek, Syrian, and Jew, all had theories about God and the world and about what was, or was not, possible. But the impossible happened; Christ returned, not as a disembodied spirit or as an animated corpse, but as a living person, wholly and completely himself.

That this is what happened is clearly implied in the New Testament accounts, and has till recently been accepted without question by the majority of those who profess to be Christians. But now we find a curious situation in which even Christians are deeply divided about what they imagine the resurrection means. One can distinguish four views which fall short, in some measure, of whole-hearted acceptance.

First come the radical Secularists who deny that there is an after-life. Such a view is indistinguishable from acknowledged agnosticism or atheism, and seems an attempt to retain some vestigial traces of religious insight while capitulating completely to the spirit of the age. Whatever its advocates maintain, this cannot be regarded as Christian belief, unless like Humpty-Dumpty they can make words mean whatever they choose. A modification of this, which amounts to the same thing, is the "objective immortality" postulated by some of Whitehead's followers. The only sense in which anyone lives on after death is as an idea in the mind of God. But this, clearly, is an immortality we do not experience. It offers no hope of righting the wrongs of earth; it is not a real victory over death.

Not quite so extreme, but equally fatal to a fully Christian world-view, is the contention of the demythologizers, led by Rudolf Bultmann, that the resurrection is not to be thought of as an event. Faith in the resurrection is faith in the cross as a saving event. To say one believes in the resurrection is to look at the cross in a particular way, a way only possible by an act of faith. In so far as one affirms Christ's victory on the cross, Christ lives on. If one asks, "How is the cross a saving event?" the answer is because it is preached as such, and this preaching elicits a response of faith, which transforms the believer's life. To this there are several objections. The most matter-of-fact is that, if the resurrection is not itself an event, but merely a way of looking at another event, namely the cross, then it is difficult, if not impossible, to account for the change in the disciples between Good Friday and Pentecost, and the consequent birth and expansion of the Church. A deeper objection is that "resurrection", so defined, is not resurrection at all. We are still dealing with a dead Christ. Though Bultmann is not a liberal in the nineteenth-century sense, in this respect at least he shares their outlook. They concerned themselves with a somewhat idealized picture of a merely human Jesus, accessible to historical research, whose "risen life" was a metaphor for his continuing historical influence. That even such an attenuated picture has inspired saints, and even martyrs, is not to be denied. But that it is an adequate account of, or explanation for, the experience of the Christian Church, I cannot believe. It is the theology of "John Brown's Body", but it is not what the disciples encountered and found themselves driven to proclaim. As Bonhoeffer says,

> Hidden in the background of this idea of Christ there lies the fact that it does not deal with the Resurrection, but only with Jesus up to the Cross, with the historical Jesus. This is the dead Christ, who can be thought of like Socrates and Goethe. Only the Risen One makes possible the presence of the living person, and gives the pre-supposition for Christology, no longer dissipated into historical energy or an inherited ideal of Christ. 5

One might add, not unfairly, that this attenuated view of Jesus and his influence could only arise and flourish in Churches whose worship puts more stress on preaching than on the sacramental life. Preaching can be itself sacramental, but it *can* become mere exhortation to remember and imitate a great figure of the past; sacraments, however, are meaningless unless they bring about an encounter with a living presence. Of all Christian Churches, it is hardly surprising that the Orthodox, with their rich liturgical life, are most vividly aware of the reality and joy of the resurrection.

The liberal faith in the Jesus of history, has led, via Schweitzer, to Bultmann's excessive scepticism about the Jesus of history. For him, what is left after historical and literary research have dealt with the New Testament, is very little indeed, and that little very doubtful. In an attempt to escape from this dependence on the historians, who seem about to destroy the very basis of the Christian faith, another school of theology has taken refuge in the concept of "salvation history". On this view, the saving acts of God are simply not accessible for secular historians to examine. At its least extreme, this view involves saying that the cross is an event in ordinary history, but that the resurrection is not, and cannot be. The resurrection is a fact accessible only to the believer, not to the historian.

That there is an element of truth in this view will become apparent, I hope, a little later. There *is* a sense in which the resurrection is not accessible except to the believer. But the appeal to two kinds of history endangers the reality of the whole enterprise. Christianity stands or falls by the irreducible element of historicity it claims to possess. Jesus is a character in our world, not in some other, semi-mythical world in which alone God is operative. The reality of redemption is rendered doubtful if all we have is, on the one hand, an ordinary man who met a tragic end, and, on the other, a story about the risen Christ. There must be some living connection between the two, or the everyday world with which history deals is left unredeemed.

The three views so far discussed fall far short of a true faith in the risen Christ. The next view does not; it accepts the resurrection, but not the empty tomb, claiming that the two can and should be distinguished and that the latter is unimportant and unbelievable. This view rests on three premisses: that even within the New Testament there is not unanimity about the empty tomb, and the evidence is at best inconclusive; that the empty tomb implies that the risen Christ was simply the dead Christ miraculously revived, and this is not what resurrection really means; and, finally, that were it true it would mean that Christ's experience was radically different from anything we can expect to happen to us, and so of no relevance to our condition. When Professor Lampe put forward this view on television at Easter, 1965, he sparked off a violent controversy in which he was quite unfairly accused of denying the most fundamental of Christian doctrines. It was clearly his intention not to deny the resurrection, but to commend it; but whether he is right to discard the empty tomb as an irrelevant and embarrassing extra, is quite another matter, which deserves further consideration.

Regarding the evidence of the New Testament, one cannot simply close one's eyes to the discrepancies between the five versions we possess, or attempt any superficial harmonizing such as would have satisfied a pre-critical age. Whether one minimizes the importance of these discrepancies, as the Archbishop of Canterbury does in *The Resurrection of Christ,* or magnifies it as

James McLeman does in *Resurrection Then and Now*, one must take them into account. Fortunately, the discrepancies, though numerous, are not all of equal importance. The most trivial are those concerning the number, and names, of the women who went to the tomb or the details of what they saw and heard. It is quite legitimate to argue both that the events of Easter Day must have been extremely confused and difficult to reconstruct afterwards, and that the accounts we have represent divergent traditions written down only after the tale had been handed on verbally, no doubt losing nothing in the telling, over a period of years. All we can then say is that something like this happened, but we cannot expect to know precisely what. One thing is clear: since the story is told entirely in terms of Palestinian burial customs, it cannot have arisen in, or even been seriously modified by, the Gentile environment into which the Christian community had moved before the Gospels were written down.

A more serious problem is the cleavage between St Matthew, who reports only an appearance in Galilee, and St Luke, who reports only events centred on Jerusalem. The divergence seems to be governed by theological presuppositions. Curiously Matthew, the Jew, wants to assure his readers that the risen Christ is to be associated with Galilee of the Gentiles, whereas Luke, the Gentile, cannot imagine the continuation of Christ's work in the Church starting anywhere but in Jerusalem. Both are making essentially the same point by means of a different symbolism; for both, the important thing is that the disciples of Christ are to take him with them to the ends of the earth, certain of his victorious power. What literal truth lies behind their choice of apparently incompatible symbolic events is difficult to say. Clearly, as they stand, they cannot be reconciled. It may be that John, who records two appearances in Jerusalem and one in Galilee, is only trying to harmonize somehow the two versions current by the end of the first century; or it may just be that he really is telling us what actually happened. It is a profound mistake to be too ready to dismiss the evidence of the Fourth Gospel as of no historical value. What *can* be dismissed is the ending of St Mark, since that is a later addition by someone who merely summarized what he found in St Luke.

What all four Gospels have in common is an empty tomb, and some message to the women to pass on to the disciples, followed later by an actual appearance of the living Jesus to one or more of the Twelve.

37

The fifth account, which is also, incidentally, the earliest, differs in making no reference to the empty tomb or to the women. This is the brief summary in 1 Corinthians 15, which St Paul gives by way of preface to his profound exploration of the meaning of the event thus attested. Lampe, and others who deny that the tomb was ever empty, make much of the fact that St Paul does not refer to it. Surely, they argue, if he had known about it he would have made something of it in trying to convince the Corinthians. To this it may fairly be answered that he is not trying to convince them but reminding them that he has convinced them; that the evidence of obscure women known personally to nobody at Corinth would in any case carry far less weight than the names of the apostles and pillars of the Church; and, finally, that although he does not mention the empty tomb he virtually implies it. Why otherwise should he stress that Christ was *buried*, and subsequently *raised*? It is far more natural to assume that he and his readers all knew about the empty tomb, and that he therefore took it for granted, than to call him as a witness *against* the tradition attested in the Gospels. It seems reasonable to conclude that while no one can reconstruct from the New Testament exactly what happened, neither has anyone the slightest grounds for picking out the disappearance of Christ's body as an inessential and expendable part of the story.

What, then, of the other grounds on which it is found incredible? It is held, first, that if Christ's physical body disappeared from the tomb and was subsequently seen by people who recognized him, this implies that his resurrection is simply a continuation of his former life, and that this is a postponement, rather than a conquest, of death. Continued existence pictured entirely in this-worldly terms is no escape from the limitations which beset us; it is rather a condemnation to endless futility. It is, however, perfectly clear that the Bible does not see Christ's risen life in these terms. In St John's Gospel a contrast is drawn between the raising of Lazarus and the resurrection of Christ. Lazarus comes forth bound hand and foot and blindfolded; freed from the grave-clothes he continues his old life, which will again end in death. Jesus passes through the grave-clothes, leaving them undisturbed, and he comes and goes at will. He is free from all limitations. Lazarus, like a case of cardiac arrest, is an instance of resuscitation to the old life, Jesus, of resurrection to a new life. Evidently it is perfectly possible to believe that Christ's resurrection involved the disappearance of his body from the tomb without inferring

38

that his risen life was subject to the limitations by which that body had previously been governed.

Lampe returns to the attack, urging that if this is what happened, then Christ's death and resurrection is radically different from ours, unless we are prepared to picture the Last Day in terms of the reassembling of our mortal remains, an idea which is now no longer tenable. In his reply to Lampe, Professor Mackinnon argued that there is a sense in which Christ was, indeed, unique. He did a work for us which we could not do for ourselves. We cannot, therefore, expect that every detail of his experience will be directly copied in ours. He is right to stress the weakness of any wholly exemplarist view of Christ's achievement, and to point out what vast and important areas of human experience lay altogether outside the scope of his incarnate life, simply because he had a work to do which excluded them. Whether this point, though a valid one, is the proper answer to Lampe's contention, I doubt. As Christians we believe that man's eternal destiny is to be pictured in terms of "resurrection" rather than just "survival" — that is to say, we believe that the only after-life of any value involves the restoration and enhancement of our whole personality rather than the continued existence — were it possible — of a part of us while the rest disintegrates and is lost. Further, it is clear from St Paul's teaching in 1 Corinthians that belief in resurrection does not, and never did, involve a belief that we shall be saddled for all eternity with our present imperfect physical equipment. Thus our risen bodies, which we shall assume at the Last Day, are not physically continuous with the bodies which will by then have disappeared utterly; and yet despite this discontinuity we shall be recognizably ourselves. If this be so, in what respect does our expectation differ from what actually happened to Christ? His body was buried, disappeared, and was replaced by a glorious and perfect body which completed and enhanced his personality, and enabled him to be recognized by those who had known him before. This is precisely what we hope will happen to us. Only the time-scale is different; that is all. We await the end of all things; but he being, as St Paul says, the first fruits, was raised to newness of life almost instantaneously.

A perfectly satisfactory case can thus be made for the contention that Christ's resurrection was an event that involved an empty tomb, even though at the same time it must be strongly asserted that his new life was more than just a continuation of the old. We cannot, however, leave the matter there and pass on to the next chapter. We have to ask, What did the resurrection prove, and to whom did it prove it? Clearly, it proved nothing to Pilate and Caiaphas. But to agree that some, then as now, could not or would not accept that it was a fact and draw the right deductions is not to admit that it could not therefore be objectively true. Much is made sometimes of the fact that Christ is said to have appeared only to his own followers, as if that made it certain that the appearances were wholly subjective. That does not follow; it is evident, on the contrary, that in most cases to see Christ was the last thing they were expecting. There is, moreover, the appearance to Saul of Tarsus, perhaps the best-attested of all. Illogically, Lampe uses the argument that Jesus was seen only by disciples to suggest that his appearance was in some sense subjective, and then reinforces this argument by taking as a typical appearance the one undoubted case of his appearing to an avowed enemy. It is apparent, certainly, that the appearance to Paul was a vision, not shared by his companions. In other words, while it was certainly an event, it was not a public event, equally accessible to all who happened to be present, but an event in the private experience of the individual to whom it occurred. It does not necessarily follow that the appearances to the other disciples were of the same kind. For one thing, if we take the New Testament at face value, the ascension had intervened. They saw the risen Lord; Paul saw the ascended Lord. Paul, therefore, could not have seen a physical presence since that had been withdrawn. His vision of Christ stands apart from all the others, and the mysterious words, "last of all to me, as to one born out of due time" (1 Cor. 15.8,AV) at first sight reinforce this impression. In fact, however, the Greek suggests *premature* birth. Using this phrase, Paul cannot have thought of Christ's appearance to him as an afterthought, a special showing for someone who had missed the original performance; on the contrary, he must have been thinking of it as a preview. He had already seen a glimpse of the glory that would be revealed when Christ returned to judge the world. If one is right to insist in this way on the strict meaning of Paul's words, then it is evident that the real uniqueness of what he had seen on the road to Damascus was not that it was a post-ascension appearance, but that it was a pre-return one. This is the only hint he gives of thinking of his experience as in any way different from that of the other disciples whose names he lists as having seen the Lord. This leaves us free to assume that, so far as he knew, what they saw was no more "objective" than what he saw. Whether a passer-by on the road to Emmaus would have seen three people or two is an unanswerable question; but it is one that hardly matters. I am inclined to agree with Lampe that the truth of the resurrection does not depend on every "appearance" being accompanied by some definite physical manifestation. What one must assert, however, is that every such appearance did involve an initiative on Christ's part and not merely a self-generated activity in the disciples' minds. It seems to me quite probable that instead of proceeding through the ordinary channels of sense-perception he made some kind of direct impact on their minds which they could not but picture as an "appearance". It is noteworthy, for instance, how often the Gospels themselves tell us that Jesus was not immediately recognized. In the Emmaus story, realization of his identity came only as he vanished. This suggests that he in some way chose the manner of his appearance, and that it was quite different from ordinary, everyday encounters.

Speculation along these lines is not, perhaps, very profitable. It is, however, worth mentioning that Professor Hooke, whose book on the resurrection was intended to be, and was hailed by a reviewer in the *Church Times* as being, a vindication of the historicity of the resurrection, quite frankly sees a parallel between what the disciples experienced and what the prophets meant when they said, "I saw the Lord". Again, as Whitehead points out in *Adventure of Ideas*: "There are external events . . . which are the normal modes of exciting sense-percepts of particular types. But . . . these external events are only the normal modes. A diet of drugs will do equally well." 6 Thus, seeing something is no guarantee that it is there. However, what one sees is not necessarily a delusion because no one else sees it. An article by Joan Fitzherbert on "Perception of Apparitions" in *The International Journal of Parapsychology* for January 1963 points out that telepathy is perfectly possible, its essence being that the mind knows that the message is generated from "without" not from "within". People with strong visual imagination form an "image" of the source of the message. Along these lines, one can account rationally for any amount of diversity in detail between different accounts of the same apparition, even if "seen" simultaneously, since, although the source of the message is genuinely external to the observers, it can only be clothed in the language and imagery of which each is capable. One can, then, maintain that Christ did in some way directly communicate with anyone he chose without this always necessarily involving an objective physical presence.

41

This seems to be how Professor Lampe pictures it, and also the more radical James McLeman. The resurrection then becomes an objective fact which can only be subjectively apprehended. This situation is not unique, and need not alarm the most orthodox Christian; it is precisely paralleled in his experience of Holy Communion where Christ is really present, but his presence can be apprehended only by faith. The point is that faith recognizes its object, it does not create it.

To picture the resurrection in this way is, I would stress, pure speculation, however plausible. It has, however, the further advantage of fitting appropriately into God's persuasive, rather than coercive, approach. Had Jesus appeared in some way that could admit of no doubt and demanded no decision and commitment on our part, he would have been untrue to the principle on which he avowedly conducted his whole mission. The difficulty of proving that he rose from the dead is precisely what we should expect, if our previous understanding of God's intentions was along the right lines. But does this mean, then, that we are no further forward, and that there is still no evidence that the love of God in Christ really did win a decisive victory on the cross? Up to a point, I am afraid it does. There can be no decisive historical verification of the resurrection, however much we would like there to be. If the tomb were proved empty, beyond a shadow of doubt, people could still avoid seeing anything significant in that: "If they hear not Moses and the prophets, neither shall they be persuaded, though one rose from the dead." A miracle is *not* some inexplicable happening which compels one to say, "This is an act of God." M.E. Glasswell, concluding a detailed study of the miracles in St Mark's Gospel, writes: "Miracles are what happens when one believes in Jesus, and it is faith in Jesus which truly perceives a miracle and by that faith that the miracles become a sign." 7 This may seem a negative conclusion. It looks as though we are being invited to take a leap in the dark. At the same time, it must be stressed that one cannot approach anything without presuppositions. The rationalist has as blind a faith as the Christian — if not, in some respects, blinder, since he is more ready to insist in advance that certain things cannot happen. Neutral history is not possible. On the evidence available it is possible to say, "Christ rose from the dead; therefore he is alive and I can hope to meet him"; it is equally possible to say, if one prefers, "The whole thing is inexplicable; perhaps something odd happened, but when you are dead, you are dead, and there is no hope." But, as David Jenkins

42

asks: "Why should the Sartrean absurdity of meaninglessness be more reasonable and acceptable than the Christian absurdity of meaningfulness?" 8 If Christ rose from the dead, this gives meaning to his life and death, and consequently to ours as well. Is not such a welcome possibility worth entertaining? We might at least suspend disbelief and give it the benefit of the doubt. If we adopt it as a tenable view, we shall find that experience will verify or falsify it for us.

Frederic Myers, a century ago, held that the resurrection would soon lose its plausibility unless it could be established that it was one of a class — that is, unless other evidence of survival could be adduced, through spiritualism and psychical research, and made scientifically convincing. I think this line of reasoning overlooks the difference between historical and scientific evidence. No historical event is ever simply one of a class. But the Christian is not entitled simply to ignore any other evidence there may be of life after death, nor is he entitled too naively to quote it to support his case. In fact, although psychical phenomena have in modern times attracted some serious scientific attention, the kind of certainty Frederic Myers hoped for has not been established, and many people are still, not without reason, entirely sceptical. Moreover, theologians have on the whole not taken such matters seriously. If they have created the impression that they are simply not interested, that is unfortunate. Orthodox Christians have, it seems to me, a variety of reasons for hesitating to investigate psychical phenomena. One is the definite biblical prohibition on consulting the spirits of the dead; though it can be argued that this is simply not relevant. Another, more cogent, is awareness of the grave risks people run in delving into the unknown, even if they only dredge up material from their own unconscious, still more if they really do establish contact with, or become possessed by, discarnate spirits whose intentions are not necessarily benevolent towards them. However, the major ground for not attaching much importance to the kind of evidence of survival popularly adduced by spiritualist mediums is that the Christian already possesses adequate evidence, which makes such dubious hints and scraps of information superfluous. The resurrection of Christ is the best attested evidence there is, not merely of survival after death, but more importantly of victory over death. Further, since the living Christ is always our contemporary, an important part of the evidence is still accessible.

Those who approach psychical phenomena in a reasonably

scientific spirit realize that for the evidence of survival to carry conviction it must satisfy certain tests. Firstly, can the dead convince us of their identity? Secondly, is there more to them than a bundle of memories? Thirdly, have they in their new environment experiences of value? Apply these tests to many — not all — instances of supposed communications from the other world and the results of the first test are inconclusive and of the third trivial. Apply these same tests to the reported appearances of the risen Christ, whose value as historical evidence we have already discussed, and we find that the appearances might have been designed to satisfy them. Christ went to considerable trouble, we are told, to identify himself to the disciples and to establish continuity with his past life: "See my hands and my feet, that it is I myself: handle me and see" (Luke 24. 39). But he is certainly not a wistful ghost exiled from earth and pining for a past life lost beyond recall. He gives the impression of being more dynamically alive than ever, and to enjoy an unbroken communion with his Father; he still has much to impart to his disciples and his appearances are designed not merely to demonstrate that he is alive but to continue their instruction and deepen their insight.

One can say, therefore, that while psychical research suggests reasonable objective tests which, on the evidence available to us, the resurrection of Christ seems to satisfy, on the other hand little or nothing has so far been discovered by such research which either confirms or modifies the accounts we have of the risen Christ. If we wish to test the reality of the Christian claim to hold the key to victory over death, it is other evidence, of a different kind, that we must seek: evidence of Christian lives, lived in this world, in which the power of the risen Christ is effectively apparent.

James McLeman ends his book on the resurrection by saying: "If I have eternal life I ought to feel it in my soul — it ought to be the life I now live by faith in the Son of God. This is how it signifies its existence; this is how it bridges the gulf that exists between the now and the not yet." 9 He seems to be making two distinct demands: "I ought to feel it in my soul", and "It ought to be the life I now live". The latter can be true even if the former is not. One may have at the moment no subjective certainty at all and yet be able to look back afterwards and see that the present life was in fact leading somewhere all the time — this is the point of John Hick's parable of the road, and of what he calls the principle of eschatological verification. When Moses asked to see God, he was told, "Thou shalt see my back parts: but my face shall not be seen" (Exod. 33. 23, AV). This can, with a little ingenuity, be taken to mean that one is never aware of the presence of God until afterwards. One never sees him coming, one only sees him going. On the road to Emmaus Jesus walked, unrecognized, beside the disciples all the way, and vanished in the very act that revealed him. This suggests that we are not to expect to see God now, but that we can expect to look back afterwards and see that he was indeed there all along. Consequently any "feeling in the soul" about eternal life, or awareness of God — and for the Bible the two things are so closely related as to be almost identical — is a very unreliable indicator. Its presence is overwhelming proof for anyone who experiences it, though not communicable as such to others; its absence is by no means a necessary demonstration of the falsity of beliefs about the presence and activity of God held on other grounds. It is, however, my contention that the resurrection of Christ does not merely open up the possibility of a life beyond death but actually transforms this present life, and this can hardly be the case if the Christian interpretation of things can *only* be eschatologically verified. In some sense it *must* be true that I can "feel it in my soul" now; otherwise, I have no particular reason for acting as if it were true, or for hoping for fuller awareness hereafter. Millions believe that they meet Christ in Holy Communion and theologians of all denominations see in that service both a proclamation of Christ's conquest of death and a foretaste of our sharing in it. In a timeless moment past, present, and future meet. But the presence of Christ in the sacrament — or anywhere else — is of a kind that cannot be demonstrated. It can only be apprehended by faith; this does not, of course, mean that it is created by faith. My faith is essential if I am to be aware of the presence of God, but that does not mean God is only there in so far as I believe him to be. This is an objective presence which can only be subjectively apprehended.

If this meeting with God in the sacrament cannot be proved to take place, how can one induce anyone to give God the opportunity of meeting him, by coming in a sufficiently expectant frame of mind? At the outset all that is required is something akin to "the willing suspension of disbelief" with which one goes to the theatre; that is, an openness to receive whatever may be there to be received. Unless one is vouchsafed some overwhelming and personally convincing revelatory experience, one must begin

45

by believing on the authority of others. One can then, on the basis of this second-hand belief, enter upon a way of life which will perhaps confirm it. Once it is thereby confirmed, the belief becomes fully one's own, now known to be true. Moreover, even if it is never convincingly confirmed in one's own experience, one must continue to give due weight to the experience of others. That Christ can change lives is demonstrated by the evidence of innumerable changed lives. That Christ can be met in this life is an assertion made by all those who can claim to have met him. Alfred Noyes once said that, if he was ever tempted to doubt the reality of the supernatural, he had only to remember the look on his father's face as he returned from early Communion. This is the kind of testimony that carries conviction. As David Jenkins remarks, "on matters of fundamental importance, persons must gain a hearing for arguments". 10 Some of us are lucky enough to have seen just such evidence of a real meeting with Christ in the lives of those near to us; but for anyone who has so far missed this experience, there is the vast range of what Dr Trevor Ling terms "first-order theology", that is, theology written out of personal experience of spiritual realities. A great deal of writing about religion is "second-order theology", a study of the writings of other people, based on no immediate awareness of one's own. The Orthodox Church restricts the term "theologian" to men who know God, we tend to apply it to men who know about men who knew God. If we want to know whether a venture of faith is worth making, it is the testimony of the poets and mystics that counts, not the arguments of academics — though the two are not necessarily mutually exclusive. Fortunately, an immense amount of first-order theology is readily accessible to the general reader, and its cumulative effect is surely enough to justify anyone not only in giving the life of faith a fair trial, but also in persevering even when the degree of subjective certainty achieved thereby is minimal.

Bishop Fison wrote, in his book, *The Christian Hope*: "the presence alone guarantees the parousia", 11 parousia being a technical term for Christ's second coming. This dictum works both ways. If the presence is necessary to give shape and content to the parousia, it is equally true that the parousia is essential if the expectation aroused by the presence, intermittent and incomplete as it always is in our experience, is ever to find satisfaction and fulfilment. The saints most aware of present communion with God are the very people who long most intensely for a future union which nothing can possibly sever. This, however, is exactly what we should expect if that understanding of the world be true which maintains that God intends us to enjoy him for ever, but has set us at a psychological distance from him in order to leave us free to make a real act of commitment and response.

. . . WE ARE RISEN

> In Him I have found the object of my desires: a personalized universe whose domination secures my personality. 1

Teilhard de Chardin

If the resurrection *did* happen, then we live in a universe where resurrection *can* happen, and the whole human situation is transformed. Since this point is fundamental, we had better stop and consider what kind of universe this must be. Many people imagine that science has made it clear that this is a closed universe with nothing detectable outside it. All events have causes within the system and are not in any demonstrable way influenced from outside; further, no evidence exists that any part of us survives death and escapes from the world of space and time. But obviously if the universe really is closed like this, then God is non-existent or unknowable, and the incarnation and the resurrection are meaningless. We may well ask if science really forces us to abandon belief both in interventions from outside and in our own destiny beyond the grave.

I am no scientist, and can go only on hearsay, but so far as I can discover, the universe as pictured by modern science is by no means as tightly sealed against all outside influence as many people suppose. It is not, to begin with, a rigidly predetermined pattern in which every event follows inexorably on its cause. Rather, an element of chance and randomness exists at the very heart of things, and what we call "laws of nature" are now seen to be statistical in character — that is, they are calculations of probabilities (usually highly reliable) based on the average performance of innumerable free agents. At any given moment, practically every item in the universe is confronted with two or more courses of action, all equally possible. At the ultra-microscopic level, chance alone governs which atom or molecule will behave in which of two possible ways; at the human level, deliberate choice may enter in. In this respect at least the universe is open, and no rigidly deterministic philosophy corresponds to the facts. 2

Then again we must beware of the "nothing but" fallacy. It

is, for instance, one thing to say that there is nothing about a living organism which in principle physics and chemistry cannot further analyse, quite another to say that the whole structure and behaviour of a living organism can be entirely explained in terms of physics and chemistry. The second statement is often taken as equivalent to the first, but in fact it does not even follow from it. It involves a quite unjustified leap. Science presents us with what Sir Peter Medawar has called "a grand hierarchy of explanations of nature". 3 A chemist can analyse everything there is in the world into a limited number of distinct components. A physicist can take the analysis even further, and ultimately see, not even matter, but only energy in various manifestations. But this kind of analysis, though it may describe accurately enough "all there is", does not account for everything, nor explain the higher stages of organization of which matter is manifestly capable. A biologist denies nothing that a chemist or physicist tells us, and in a way he adds nothing; but he is able to make better sense of living beings by a descriptive analysis which rests on, and presupposes, the fundamental laws of physics and chemistry and yet goes far beyond them. A psychologist will go further, and accepting all that can be said about living beings by a biologist, add another level of description and explanation which applies to sentient and responsive beings. History and the social sciences go further still and deal with the interactions of sentient beings within a given environment. At each level the description is complete as far as it goes, and yet leaves out something which only a higher level of explanation can deal with. A fully-integrated explanation of every conceivable phenomenon is probably utterly beyond our capacity to achieve or even imagine, but obviously such an all-embracing explanation, if it exists, would not take the form of a reduction of everything to the "nothing but physics" level; but would have to take account of every subsequent degree of improbability and complexity. The claim of theology to be "the queen of the sciences" rested on its supposed ability to give just such an over-arching and all-embracing explanation, and though the claim has long been so vigorously disputed as to cause its tacit abandonment, for the Christian it is still, in a sense, true. Nothing can, in fact, be completely explained without bringing in God; but this does not amount to a proof of his reality. Many people are content to rest in partial and incomplete explanations, and leave the problem of how they fit together as an impenetrable mystery. The Christian has to admit that they may be right; but he is entitled to demand, in return, a clear recognition that the nature of the physical universe is not such as definitely to exclude God. It is not totally and utterly self-explanatory in terms of discoverable impersonal laws. There is room for God; but that there is a God can be established only if he himself chooses to make his presence felt.

Evidently in a universe such as we have just been picturing, miracle is not ruled out *a priori*. Since nothing is rigidly predetermined, the utterly unlikely *may* happen at any time, and since none of our levels of explanation is complete in itself, events may occur which are perfectly rational when viewed from above and yet seem totally inexplicable when seen from below. This does not, of course, justify anyone in accepting without further explanation every alleged miracle at its face value; but it does mean that if we come upon one as well-attested as the resurrection it is not irrational to suspend disbelief. It perhaps also implies that we should look upon such miracles not as *exceptions* but as *examples* – particularly striking manifestations of God's essential nature and activity, rather than interventions in, and interruptions of, the normal course of events. F.D. Maurice was among the first to advocate this approach to them. In his commentary on St John, he wrote of Jesus, "He did not come into the world to break God's laws, but to establish them, and to show forth the will which was at the foundation of them." 4

At any given moment if we take a slice through the universe, it shows layer upon layer of increasing complexity; but the total pattern has, of course, a fourth dimension, that of time. The universe is not static, but in constant process of alteration and development. The higher levels of complexity we now see have only gradually emerged. The discovery of evolution has brought home to us that everything has a history, and can only be understood when its history is taken into account. Teilhard de Chardin, in *The Phenomenon of Man*, made a gargantuan attempt to see and describe the total pattern; from the raw material of the universe, the stuff of physics and chemistry, first life evolved, and then thought. To him it is no optical illusion that man, looking around the world, naturally sees everything with himself at the centre; the lines really do converge on him. Man is the highest point that evolution has yet reached, and the spearhead of further advance. "The universe is a collector and conservator, not of mechanical energy, as we supposed, but of persons." 5 Although Teilhard's work has been dismissed by

Medawar as "poetistic nonsense", this is surely a reasonable way of looking at things. The "nothing but" school tries, unsuccessfully, to explain everything in terms of the constituents out of which it has evolved; Teilhard tries to explain evolution not in terms of origins but in terms of destination. To refuse to accept such an attempt as legitimate is to say that the whole process is random and fortuitous, and this surely requires the greater degree of credulity. If Teilhard is right, we are back in a universe every bit as personal as the mythological one, dominated by angels and demons, which Christians are now urged to abandon. Quality, not quantity, is the decisive factor; vast aeons of time and the immensities of space have provided a backcloth for the production of thinking beings. A universe in which personality can emerge at all must surely be a universe designed to produce personality. If we argue that God could have achieved this result a good deal more quickly and economically, the answer is perhaps to be found along the lines explored in chapter 2 above. We are placed in this vast universe so as to be given the opportunity for development, for free choice, and for a loving response to our Creator. We are at the summit of the evolutionary tree because in us, at last, a free response is possible. But the whole apparatus is necessary because without it the conditions in which such freedom can be exercised would not exist.

A further point follows, if this is right. Once granted that the collection and conservation of persons is what the universe is *for,* death cannot have the last word or the purpose would, after all, be frustrated. Therefore some kind of survival is called for. We can even define a little more precisely what kind of survival is required. We cannot, of course, describe it, since it lies at present outside our experience and any language we apply to it must be analogical. Hence the absolute necessity of mythology and poetry in any attempt to convey to the human imagination some idea of the quality of the after-life. What we can say, quite unequivocally, is that if survival is to be a meaningful conclusion to the story as we see it now, then it must satisfy two conditions. It must somehow be a survival of the whole personality of each of us, and it must involve us all together, not some of us in isolation. These two conditions correspond, in fact, to two fundamental articles of Christian belief — the resurrection of the body and the communion of saints. These beliefs arose out of a Jewish way of looking at man and his world, and were confirmed for Christians by the resurrection of Jesus and the corporate

51

experience of the Church; but they also correspond to the modern world-view and its demands better than any other doctrine of human survival after death. The coincidence, surely, is too remarkable to be an accident.

The first condition follows from what has been said about the structure of the physical universe. Where the "nothing but" school are right is in contending that all the higher structures do have a physical base. At each level we co-ordinate units into more and more complex wholes; but we are not adding anything new. If I say "I decided to do such and such", and if a physiologist gives a complete account of what is going on in my brain, we are talking about the same thing in different ways; there is not a separate parallel activity of deciding going on while the nerve-cells carry on their business at a merely physical level. The "I" that thinks and feels is real; but it is not a different entity from the one that can for certain purposes be studied as a mechanical system. The point can perhaps be illustrated by thinking of a painting. One can give a complete and exhaustive account of it as a physical object; one can examine it minutely, brush-stroke by brush-stroke; one can even analyse the pigments chemically. But only by standing back and looking at it as a whole can one see what it is meant to represent. That does not mean that the picture is something added to the paint, but it is something one can only see by not looking exclusively *at* the paint. If one destroyed the painting, one would have destroyed the picture along with the paint. The meaning is not separable from the medium used to express it. If this is a fair analogy, one cannot destroy the physical framework in which the mind does its thinking and feeling and claim that it makes no difference. Man is not to be likened to a letter in an envelope, the envelope necessary only to ensure the arrival of the letter at its destination, and then to be discarded while what it held is preserved intact. The essential "I" cannot survive unless in some sense the machinery survives as well. But bodies do disintegrate beyond hope of reintegration, and in any case they are imperfect and impermanent, so this looks like an argument for the impossibility of survival. However, human beings differ from paintings in several important respects. They are dynamic, developing, living creatures, and are never completed and finished in the way that a painting is. All through their lives the physical organism, to say nothing of the less tangible elements of memory and character, are undergoing constant change. All the parts can be replaced over and over again, and yet the same entity somehow survives. After death it is clearly necessary that there be some degree of continuity and some form of embodiment; but the reassembly of every particle of the physical body exactly as it was at the moment of death is not necessary for this. It is true that belief in the resurrection of the body has been held by eminent Christians in a crudely materialistic form; but a careful look at 1 Corinthians 15 will show that St Paul clearly did not take it that literally. All that is necessary for continued personal identity is that my memory-traces and dispositional traits be somehow preserved or recreated, and transferred to some more durable material than the grey-matter inside my skull. But they must be *mine*, or *I* do not survive. What this involves is something akin to transferring a recording from a tape to a disc. This does not seem to be an utterly impossible process to imagine, and Christ's resurrection suggests that it has happened and can, therefore, happen again. As we have seen, his rising from the dead involved both physical discontinuity and a continuity of personal identity. Survival, then, is to be pictured not as the lingering-on after death of some intangible aspect of an irretrievably dismembered personality, but as the reintegration at some future date of all that made that person alive and unique. "Resurrection of the body" is not only more biblical than "immortality of the soul", it also makes better sense in terms of our modern understanding of human nature. It has the further consequence of making quite clear that this is no automatic process, which might have come about by chance, or which any of us can take for granted. The recalling from oblivion of a personality every aspect of which is by nature perishable depends on a direct and deliberate intervention by God.

The second consideration is based on another evident fact about man as such. Just as he is firmly rooted in the material world, so is he essentially a social animal. A purely spiritual existence would be less than human; so would an entirely solitary one. If we survive at all, we need social contacts. Our chief such contact will of course be with God, and some argue that this in itself will be such an overwhelming and utterly satisfying experience as to leave no room for any kind of awareness of other people; but I do not find this convincing. In this life our relations with other people are valuable for their own sake, and also as ways in which the experience of God is mediated and shared. If we imagine that these relations and interactions will cease when we are dead, are we not virtually saying that we shall cease to be

53

human? "There you shall enjoy your friends again that are gone hither before you; and there you shall with joy receive even every one that follows into the holy place after you." Bunyan's moving words *must* be true, if life after death is to be anything we can recognize as life

Man's life on earth is, and always has been, entirely conditioned by belonging to a group. Man, though he can endure solitude if necessary, is not a natural solitary. At first, indeed, it seems that he had only a very rudimentary self-awareness. The individual was nothing, the group everything. Individual survival after death was of no great interest, so long as the tribe continued to exist, and the individual shared thereby in a kind of corporate and this-worldly immortality.

Even in the Old Testament, full as it is of vivid and colourful individuals, the concern is mainly with the Chosen People as a whole and their historical destiny, and the hope of the individual, such as it is, lies in the good fortune of happening to belong to the most favoured nation. It has been argued that the Greek city states saw the first emergence of real individualism:

> They gave scope to individuals by freeing them from the bonds of Nature worship — above all, from the particularly cramping bonds of the worship of Nature in the form of the family. Family life holds mankind in bondage to non-human Nature. In the bosom of the family, human beings are not independent personalities, with minds and wills of their own; they are twigs of a family tree, which, in turn, is a branch of the evolutionary tree of life whose roots reach down into the abyss of the sub-conscious psyche. 6

It is, however, only in modern times, since the rise of science and the technology based on it, that there has been for the majority of mankind any extensive desacralization of nature and society. Christianity has often settled down and been thoroughly at home in a sacral society, such as the Byzantine Empire and its Russian successor, which survived to within living memory; and many Christians have viewed the process of desacralization with regret and alarm. Others argue that it is a good thing; that only by being freed from enslavement to false gods can man achieve his full stature as a son of God; and that the process is one which biblical religion demanded and initiated. Certainly the Old Testament prophets waged an unremitting war against the tendency to deify nature; certainly, the Bible contains the promise that man should subdue and control nature, and this is only now being

54

fulfilled; certainly, modern science arose in a Christian context and it can be argued that it could not have arisen in any other. But the radicals who rejoice amid this triumph of secularization tend to overplay their hand and talk as if "religion" and "the sacred" can, should, and will disappear utterly from human life. I see secularizing as a necessary stage in human development, but not as the final stage. There is much that Christians can and should welcome about modern society, variously described as open, plural, and permissive. The Christian Church is a voluntary body; it can only be joined, in any meaningful sense, by a free act of individual personal commitment. Therefore Christianity needs for its full flowering an environment in which individuals are free to make choices and this is what modern society is at least supposed to supply. As a missionary situation, the plural society has the advantage every time over a sacral society. Here is an environment in which free, personal faith can develop. Here, too, is an environment in which men of different faiths or of none can meet and communicate as never before. If society is genuinely open, then the opportunities for Christian missionary activity are greater than ever before, though the commending of the faith is no longer made deceptively easy by social pressures in favour of conformism. It could be argued that it is the Christian's duty to be on his guard to ensure that society is indeed genuinely open and really does allow and encourage individual freedom. It is in the interest of Christianity to campaign for real, rather than illusory, freedom; for to be itself the Church requires members who have freely and willingly joined.

I have assumed that the Church can and should accept a plural and secular society, but that it still has a reason for existing apart from, and even over against, society at large. Why is this? Because pluralism is only a stage on the way to unity, and because the Church is, at least in intention, the germ of a new kind of community which will unify the human race; not only is such a community the next stage in human evolution; unless it is achieved, the human race is likely to perish. The movement hitherto has been from a community in which the individual is submerged to a state of affairs in which the individual asserts himself even at the expense of the community of which he is a part, and which he needs for his own development. What is needed is a community in which the individual, so far from being lost, can at last find himself. The Church's aim is to bring more and more people into a living relationship with each other and with God, so as to form just such a community, coextensive within the whole race and yet fully satisfying to each individual. God's loving purpose involves of necessity leaving us free to choose; but that freedom has achieved its purpose only if we choose to respond to love with love. The end is not anarchic individualism, but the willing acceptance of certain ties.

In this context, Whitehead's analysis of the evolution of religion is relevant. He is often attacked by Christians, full of zeal for the Church, for saying, "Religion is what an individual does with his own solitariness." But that oft-quoted dictum needs to be seen in its context; primitive religion is merely social and unreflective, and religion in its decline tends to sink back into mere sociability — an observation which is easily verified by examining certain features of contemporary parish life. But in between comes the emergence of the individual consciousness from the primitive collective; and it is the individual and his reflection on the universe, in solitude, that is the basis of all the world's higher religions. Again, all the great figures in the Bible, together with the Buddha and Mohammed, seem to bear out the truth of this observation. But the individual's reflections, if they are of any consequence at all, do not remain his private affair. If he believes them to be true, he will try to ensure that they are universally accepted. So the religious insights of the individual become the foundation of a new kind of community, a community joined by choice and not by birth, and extended by persuasion rather than force. This does not seem to me to be in any sense an attack on organized religion, though it does define with some clarity what kind of community it ought to produce; and it must be admitted that the Church has not always had a very clear insight into its own essential nature.

The point of the kind of community towards which we are aiming is not the extinction of individuality but the full flowering of personality. As Fr Paul Singleton puts it: "We used to define a person in terms of individuality and uniqueness. Today, while not denying these truths, we stress the fact that man is a person because he can enter into relationships with other persons; that as well as existing for himself, he also exists for other people." 7 The full development of the individual's personality depends, then, on his being a member of a society. For Christians this is true, in a sense, even of God, who is not a remote, isolated *individual*, but a family or group. As David Jenkins remarks: "The reality to which the symbol of the Trinity points is highly relevant to that balance of the individual, the relational and the communal in which the fulfilment of personalness may be looked for." 8 Self-awareness and awareness of others are necessary to each other, they are two sides of the same coin. Clearly, no form of survival beyond death is satisfactory which goes back on this understanding of man and allows the individual to sink without trace into some undifferentiated whole, like a drop of water in the ocean. But survival pictured in too individualistic a way does equal violence to human nature. Fred Hoyle, misunderstanding Christian doctrine in this way, thought it offered him an eternity of frustration shut up in his own self-hood. He wanted instead to see "an evolution of life whereby the essence of each of us becomes welded together into some vastly larger and more potent structure". 9 But this, according to Teilhard de Chardin is just what Christianity does offer him.

Teilhard seems to have been suggesting that humanity is moving towards some kind of "superperson" in which the individual human being will be a cell, albeit a sentient one. The idea attracts, because it suggests some goal for the evolutionary process, which has obviously not yet reached perfection, and at the same time offers a new way of looking at such ideas as the body of Christ and the communion of saints. But it must not be pressed to the point where the individual loses his identity in the race. This would not be going on, but turning back. In the course of the world's history new things have emerged — life from lifeless matter, rationality from pre-rational creatures — but the new has not destroyed or violated the old, but rather presupposed it. Human beings are subject to physical and biological laws, even though they form a higher order of being subject to psychic laws which do not apply to the lower levels. Evolution always builds on the foundation of what has gone before. Now that personality has emerged, no further step forward can be envisaged that would destroy personality. The kind of community implied in such concepts as the Body of Christ or Teilhard's "superperson" is not one in which the individual counts for less than he does now.

The resurrection of Christ is a step forward in evolution comparable to the emergence of life or of reason. It has made a difference not only to our future hopes but to our present condition. The "superperson" already exists, albeit in a rudimentary form, since Christ has left behind him a human embodiment, the Church, which is in process of becoming the new community in which humanity will achieve its destiny in the purpose of God. This, as we shall see in a moment, is the contention of the New Testament, and it is clearly a dangerous one to put forward, since it can be put to some sort of test. Christianity could render itself immune from any kind of falsification by making assertions only about what we can expect to experience in another world; but in fact at its best it is prepared to run the risk of making assertions that can be verified or falsified in terms of present experience. If it is found to be justified, then what it offers is not merely "pie in the sky when you die" but a radical transformation of our present situation. Even the lesser assertion would not be without value. This life, pictured solely as a vale of tears, would be infinitely more bearable if we could be convinced of the reality of a beyond in which all wrongs would be righted. But in fact Christianity offers here and now a foretaste of that other life, and tangible evidence that it exists.

If we had only Paul's speeches in Acts, and especially those before his judges, we might be excused for imagining that his gospel did hinge on what happens when we die. He aligned himself adroitly with the Pharisees against the Sadducees, asserting that he was on trial because he believed in the resurrection of the dead, and offered new evidence of the truth of Israel's hope by pointing to the fact of Christ's return from the dead. On this view Christ, "the first to rise from the dead" (Acts 26. 23, RSV) is one of us, chosen by God to demonstrate the truth of something for which we all long — a meaningful existence beyond the grave.

But this, though certainly part of Paul's teaching, is by no means the heart of it. With a sure grasp of essentials the Church has appointed for the Epistle on Easter Day part of the third chapter of his Epistle to the Colossians, which begins, "If ye then be risen with Christ, seek those things which are above". . . In this passage, he goes on to assert unhesitatingly, "ye are dead, and your life is hid with Christ in God". This is axiomatic, and upon it all his advice to Christians is based. Nor is this passage unique and isolated. Close parallels can be found in other Epistles ascribed to St Paul, and similar ideas are expressed in other ways elsewhere in the New Testament.

The train of thought in Colossians is as follows. Christians have died with Christ, and now share with him a new life which is at present "hid with God", not openly manifest. But it will in due course be fully revealed, and in the meantime it is absolutely necessary to make a complete break with the old life. As the

Jerusalem Bible puts it, "kill everything in you that belongs only to earthly life" (Col. 3. 5, JB). One of the things to be thus discarded is the old rule-bound morality. The old self has been stripped off, to be replaced by a new self – the real, undistorted self, in the image of the Creator. Because of this refashioning in God's image there is no room for distinctions between different kinds of human being – Jews and Greeks, slaves and free, civilized and barbarian (we might nowadays add white and coloured). "There is only Christ, he is everything and he is in everything" (Col. 3. 11, JB).

Here we have a biblical basis for the idea of a new all-embracing community transcending all the bitter divisions that separate men from each other, a community which can in some sense be described as a superperson, because ultimately there is only Christ. And this community is put forward not as a possibility, but as an actuality, brought into being by Christ's death and resurrection. Romans 7 offers a close parallel to Colossians 3. Christians through the body of Christ are now dead to the law and consequently are freed by death from their imprisonment, free to serve in the new spiritual way. The new freedom is not to be equated with unchecked individualism, since it is freedom within a community, and Paul always goes on to lay down the norms of behaviour which must be accepted and complied with if the community is not to be utterly wrecked. But this is not substituting one legalism for another; it is replacing the letter by the Spirit, the external by the internal, law by love.

Ephesians may or may not be by St Paul; but it moves within the same world of thought. In the second chapter we find first the assertion "you were dead". What "being dead" means we gather from chapter 4, which refers to the aimless kind of life pagans live, estranged from the life of God. From this death, caused by sin, God brought us to life with Christ, raising us with him and giving us a place with him in heaven. The implication of Christ's resurrection is taken to be, not that we *shall* go to heaven, but that we *are* in heaven already. Therefore follows the exhortation to give up our old way of life completely and set aside our old self.

When St Paul speaks of a present enjoyment of the risen life, he links it with an experience which every believer has already undergone, and which he describes in terms of death and rebirth – the experience of conversion and baptism. He does not distinguish clearly between them, as in the early Church they went together. His teaching about baptism is that it does involve some kind of sharing in Christ's death and resurrection. "When we were baptised, we went into the tomb with him, and joined him in death, so that as Christ was raised from the dead by the Father's glory, we too might live a new life" (Rom. 6. 3-4, JB). It follows, "you must consider yourselves to be dead to sin, but alive for God in Christ Jesus" (Rom. 6. 11, JB). As an eighteenth-century writer summed it up, "When Christians go to heaven they are not carried into a new society for they are already by the grace of God translated into it by baptism." 10

When Paul described baptism in terms of death and rebirth he was not being at all far-fetched. When, in the early days of Christianity, an adult came to be baptized and renouncing his past life stripped off his old garments and went down naked under the waters, emerging naked on the far side, to be clothed in a new white robe, death and birth were vividly enacted. And for the candidate himself this was no charade, but a decisive act, which involved cutting himself off from his past associates and committing himself irrevocably to a new and highly dangerous way of life. The sense in which this could be called "dying to the world" was all too obvious. Again, in a hostile world, Christians formed, of necessity, a close-knit community. Hence being baptized is not an individual experience; it leads to fellowship. A corollary of baptism for Paul is receiving the Spirit of God, and that Spirit is a Spirit of *fellowship*. According to 1 Cor. 12. 13, what now unites Jews, Greeks, slaves, and free men in a single family is that they all by baptism share the same Spirit. Later theology was to see a close parallel between the way in which Father and Son are united in the One Spirit, in the holy and undivided Trinity, and the way in which mankind is by the same Spirit brought into the unity of God's family. Such thinking finds its biblical basis in St John as well as in St Paul.

Can we, however, still accord the same significance to baptism in a world where in countries formerly Christian the vast majority of the population are still baptized as a matter of course, even though their baptism is rarely followed by any positive commitment to Christ? This kind of indiscriminate baptism is very hard to justify, though the baptism of the children of believers is a perfectly reasonable proceeding. In some ways infant baptism symbolizes what is going on even better than adult baptism; it emphasizes, for instance, that God's grace always precedes our response, and that baptism, being but our birth into a new life, must be followed by growth. Certainly for the modern Christian who cannot even remember his baptism, it is difficult to accord it the decisive significance St Paul gives to it. There are, apparently, two ways of becoming a Christian. In Rosemary Sutcliff's historical novel, *Sword at Sunset*, the hero describes how, with much patience — though he was himself wounded at the time — he won over and tamed a magnificent dog that had belonged to a dead enemy. When the dog finally abandoned its pride and came to him, he says,

> It was a little like the moment in the taming of horse or hawk, when the wild thing that has been fighting you with all its wild nature, fighting to the point of heartbreak for both of you, suddenly accepts, and gives of its free will what it has struggled so long to withhold. (For the thing is always in the end, in the essence, a free yielding by the beast, never a forced conquest by the man. With a dog, in the normal way, it is different, for a dog is born into man's world, and tries from the first to understand.) 11

Here, it seems to me, is an apt and striking picture of the two ways of becoming a Christian. One, the experience St Paul underwent and wrote about, is the climax of a mounting struggle. It is a kind of death, and only by going through it can one come to the new life. The other way, the way normal for domestic animals and the children of believing parents, is to grow gradually into a deepening relationship, starting from an acknowledged and confident dependence, and trying always to grow in understanding. Neither way is better than the other, and no one can be forced to make his developing relationship with God fit into a stereotyped pattern. Both, of course, presuppose a Christian community, into which we are welcomed, or in which we are reared. The continuing community is the essential background for all varieties of individual experience. It is within the community that a relationship with God can develop, and it is the extra dimension given by such a relationship that matters. Whether or not we can recall any experience of rebirth, we are all, as Christians, expected to know what it means to lead a new life. That is to say being a Christian should add a new dimension to life so vivid and important that life without it seems like death.

All too often Christian belief is pictured in terms which seem to be derived from the Acts, without the deeper insights made explicit in the Epistles. Our sure and certain hope of resurrection is held to rest on a sure and certain fact in the past — the resurrection of Christ — but it seems to make very little difference to the present. Christ is imagined as having risen from the dead and, after being seen by a few people for a short time, as having returned to heaven, where he is now, remote from the world we know. One day, either he will return to us on earth or we shall go to him in heaven. This parody of Christianity is encouraged by such hymn verses as:

> So age by age, and year by year
> His grace was handed on;
> And still the holy church is here
> *Although her Lord is gone.*   12

What the hymn-writer takes in his stride, the poet sees as tragic:

> Whatever being passed
> Beyond that holy shroud into the mind of God
> No longer sees this earth: we are alone.   13

But, in fact, such a doctrine of the "real absence" of Christ from the world cannot be justified from the New Testament. At first sight it seems reasonable to interpret the ascension in this way, but it is not the only way, and another hymn gives us a truer insight into its significance for us:

> Thou hast raised our human nature
> In the clouds to God's right hand;
> There we sit in heavenly places,
> There with thee in glory stand;
>
> Jesus reigns, adored by Angels;
> Man with God is on the throne;
> Mighty Lord, in thine Ascension
> We by faith behold our own.   14

It is quite true that in the New Testament the ascension marks the end of the *appearances* of the risen Christ (apart from exceptional occasions such as the conversion of St Paul) but this in no way implies the withdrawal of his *presence*. His last words in St Matthew's Gospel are "Lo I am with you always, even unto the end of the world" (Matt. 28. 20, AV), and St Luke implies that the Acts of the Apostles is an account of all Jesus *continued* to do and teach. The Church is not the steward of an absentee land-lord, but the agency through which he makes his presence felt. What brings the Church into being and keeps it together is the

Spirit of Christ — according to St Luke first poured out at Pentecost, according to St John a direct gift of the risen Christ on Easter Day. The withdrawal of Christ's physical presence makes possible a new kind of indwelling presence, which is mediated, or guaranteed by the Spirit. He does not replace Christ, but provides the necessary medium for Christ's continuing activity. The Christian creeds link together the Church, the communion of saints, baptism, forgiveness, resurrection, and eternal life in the paragraph which deals with the person and work of the Holy Spirit. There is a genuine and intimate connection between these apparently disparate items. The Spirit of Christ is the Spirit of fellowship whose activity brings men together into a community where they experience release from their failures and frustrations and come to see a meaning in life which positively demands that death be transcended. Being a Christian is a profoundly personal experience which is self-authenticating, and yet it is an experience available within a defined community, the Church, and mediated by certain rites, the sacraments. In the New Testament it appears to be available exclusively through these means; the Bible is unable to picture solitary Christians, and is silent on the position and prospects of conscientious non-joiners, or the unfortunates who have had no opportunity of contact with Christ in his mystical and sacramental body. These are grave limitations. I, for one, do not believe that the eternal destiny of all men depends exclusively on sacramental incorporation in the visible Christian community on earth; but I think it is at least arguable that it is only by this means that one can on earth escape from the futility and meaninglessness of existence, and come into undoubted contact with the power behind the universe, the power that set the seal of victory on Christ's ministry by raising him from the dead.

This is how one of the Fathers links together the element in the third paragraph of the Creed:

After confessing the Holy Trinity, thou goest on to profess that thou believest in *the Holy Catholic Church*. What else is the Church than the congregation of all saints? From the beginning of the world, be it patriarchs, Abraham, Isaac, and Jacob, prophets, apostles, martyrs, or all other just men who have been, are, or shall be, are one Church because they are sanctified by one faith and life, sealed by one Spirit, made one body; of which body the head is held to be Christ, as indeed it is written [Eph. I. 22; 5. 23; Col. 1. 18]. I go further. Even angels, virtues and powers supernal are united in this one

Church; for the Apostle teaches that *in Christ all things are reconciled, whether things on earth or things in heaven* [Col. 1. 20]. So in this one Church thou believest that thou art able to attain *the Communion of Saints.* 15

He goes on to warn the convert to beware of inferior imitations. The true Church has, unfortunately, a number of rivals. Such teaching exhibits an apparent contradiction between the utmost inclusiveness and the strictest exclusiveness. The Church is for all men, and all good men belong to it already; yet one has to be very careful to make sure that what one belongs to is the Church of God, and not some merely human institution which offers not life, but death. It is perhaps worth exploring what it means to talk about "the communion of Saints". In the Bible sanctity and holiness are not basically moral qualities; a saint is not a person of heroic virtue. To be holy means to be set apart for God. Things used by God are holy; and so are people used by God. It is, I think, impossible to eliminate from biblical religion the distinction between sacred and secular. The world is organized apart from God, in neglect or defiance of God. Things and people must be detached from a false allegiance to the world, and find their true allegiance to God. They must, in fact, be transferred from the secular to the sacred. It is not the sacred that is destined to disappear, but the secular. In due course the whole creation must and shall revolve around its true centre; in the meantime, individuals escaping from death to life must go against the crowd. There is nothing exclusive in intention about the Church — quite the reverse — but the way in is necessarily narrow.

It is when we remember the essentially temporary nature of the temporal order as we know it now that the apparent oddities and contradictions of New Testament teaching fall into place. On the one hand, our death and resurrection are past facts, over and done with already, and the new life can be lived and enjoyed now. On the other hand, there is still urgency about the demand to give up our old life, and there is still an immense enrichment of our present experience to be looked for in the future. This is only to be expected, since Christians are still in the world, still subject to all its pressures and temptations, and only death will release them from these. Hence the ambivalence of death — to the godless, it is the last word in futility, whereas for those who are being redeemed it is the final breakthrough into life. As F.D. Maurice pointed out, in one of his sermons on St John:

Life has a relation to joy, which is as close as the relation of death to sadness. Our minds become confused on this point. We talk of the burden of life. We talk of death as delivering us from this burden. But these are careless expressions, against which the conscience of man rebels. The Scripture is in harmony with the conscience. It speaks of our carrying about with us a burden of *death,* from which we need to be delivered. If it ever speaks of the moment of departure from the world as a moment of deliverance, it is because as the poet says, "Death itself here dies". 16

Christians already belong to the world they will only fully enter when death releases them from this world. They are "a colony of heaven" (Phil. 3. 20); they are "strangers and pilgrims" (1 Pet. 2. 11); like Abraham they "seek their real homeland" (Heb. 11. 14). To the first generation this unexpected overlapping of two worlds seemed so odd that it could not possibly last long; to us, after two thousand years, it is the normal state of affairs. Yet it is still odd and unsatisfactory, and leads to confusion and paradox. Christians have to be exhorted to "become what they are".

Why this should be can perhaps be accounted for like this. We have passed, so far as human beings are concerned, the stage of genetical evolution. In us evolution has become conscious. Any further steps forward cannot just take place without our knowledge and consent. Thus, although the possibility of a new dimension of living is open to us, and has been available for the better part of two thousand years, it is up to each of us to decide whether to take the opportunity or whether to carry on in the old way. It is becoming increasingly clear that the old way is a way of death, futile, aimless, and destructive. It is also all too clear that man cannot unaided give a new direction to evolution or a new dimension to his individual and corporate life, however much he may long to, and however many secular prophets exhort him to do so. Only by grace can we be saved. But grace does not override nature. We can be helped only with our consent. We can be set on the right path; but we must make the effort to keep on it. Hence, while God's decisive intervention has broken open the closed universe in which we felt ourselves imprisoned, and liberated us from every man-made shackle, it is still up to us whether we stay in the prison or exercise our perilous liberty. This accounts for the curious mixture of assertion and exhortation in the New Testament.

As for the tension between the "now" and the "not yet" which

65

is equally characteristic of the New Testament, that arises surely from the fact that we are watching in ourselves and in the world the slow unfolding of a process whose full flowering the universe itself, finite as it is, will not be able to contain. The new life in Christ is only in its infancy; its adulthood is almost beyond our imagining, though we know enough already to look forward to the rest with longing. St Paul found himself obliged both to assert that Christians are already dead to the world and share Christ's hidden life and also to reprove those who held that the general resurrection was past. Evidently some converts misunderstood him to mean that, since Christ had died and they by baptism had shared his death, they would not have to die in the ordinary sense at all. The death of baptized believers was a great shock to the Christian community, notably at Thessalonica. Paul insisted that the resurrection was still to come, and that, even if we chanced to be alive on the last day, we should need to undergo a radical transformation; our present bodies are not intended for eternal life. None the less, eternal life can be experienced now. The clue to this lies in the biblical understanding of death and life. Life without God *is* death. Paul talks of dying to the world, but really it is the world that is dead. Existence estranged from God is deadly — limited, hopeless, without meaning or purpose, and utterly frustrating. Conversely, even the slightest awareness of God opens the door to a new life. Our awareness of God in this life is fitful and intermittent, but it does give purpose and meaning and hope. This is undoubtedly "life from the dead", however we may long for a clearer vision and a steadier purpose.

The new life, if it is to be really worth while, must have two aspects. It must secure for us a genuine communion with God, and it must make possible an undistorted relationship between men. The phrase, "the communion of saints", implies both aspects: the Godward, since a *saint* is one set apart from God; the manward, since it is a *communion*, a fellowship, which is God-given and not man-made and therefore satisfactory and lasting. The way in which this fellowship is called into being becomes clearer when we remember that in the original languages in which the creeds were written *the communion of saints* can be either masculine or neuter — that is, it can refer either to the fellowship of God's people, or to the sharing in holy things. The two belong together inseparably, because it is through the sacraments that Christ brings the Church into being and sustains its life. It is in the sacraments that we can be most certain of meeting the living Christ for ourselves, and hence of proving to ourselves that he really is risen.

It is evident that, if one concentrates in this way on Church and sacraments and tries to find in their actual empirical reality some evidence that Christ is alive, one enormous aspect of the communion of saints will be virtually ignored. We have been concentrating on our experience in time, and the grounds it gives us for supposing time can be transcended. But one of the things this doctrine stands for is the fact that the Christian community is not, even now, restricted to living Christians. The living, the departed, and the unborn belong together in one communion and fellowship; mutual intercession is the lifeblood of the fellowship. If Christ has really conquered death, then death cannot be an insuperable barrier between a man and his departed relations and friends. Christians do not need to turn to spiritualist mediums or psychical researchers, to be convinced of what they already know.

This point is stressed by John Taylor, in his book, *The Primal Vision,* which is concerned with the Christian presence in African tribal religion. The African is very much aware of his dead. Christianity offers his departed the prospect of life, rather than the earthbound and frustrating existence he has hitherto imagined for them. It ought also to offer the living a stronger, rather than a weaker, sense of solidarity with departed generations and, in Christ, a readier and more intimate contact. A similar challenge confronts Christians in the Far East: the Chinese no more worship their ancestors than Roman Catholics worship saints. Respect and affection shown to departed members of the family, and continued concern for their welfare, ought never to be dismissed out of hand as idolatrous. Such an attitude should be taken up and shared by Christians, quite naturally, but on a sounder theoretical basis. Unfortunately, in Western Christianity, Catholicism has built up an elaborate and artificial picture of the after-life, inadequately grounded in Scripture and presumptuous in appearing to know too much. Protestantism reacts to this with indignant rejection or embarrassed silence. On the whole, only the Orthodox are able to set an example of natural and unselfconscious communion with the dead in Christ. They are still members of the family, to be prayed for and asked to pray for us; as a Quaker once put it, "the incident of death puts no boundaries to the Blessed Community". 17

It is the well-attested experience of the Christian community that death does not, in fact, sever Christ's followers from each other, but that in his presence we all meet day by day. John Betjeman gives this poignant expression in his picture of the clergyman's widow:

> Now all the world she knew is dead
>   In this small room she lives her days
> The wash-hand stand and single bed
>   Screened from the public gaze. . . .
> Now when the bells for eucharist
>   Sound in the Market Square
> With sunshine struggling through the mist
>   And Sunday in the air,
> The veil between her and her dead
>   Dissolves and shows them clear,
> The consecration prayer is said,
>   And all of them are near.   18

There are difficulties about this experience, when one stops to analyse it. If one believes, not in inherent immortality but in a resurrection initiated by God, then it is natural that it is only in God that we should meet and recognize our dead, but the biblical view does suggest a hiatus between death and resurrection during which the dead can be described as sleeping. The only way we can picture them as already glorified, already made whole and aware of themselves, of God, and of us, is to assume that the categories of time do not apply beyond the grave, but that they, with God, live now in an eternal present. This is not, in itself, implausible.

However, since we cannot possibly *know* anything about the after-life, or even imagine it very convincingly until we die, it is perhaps better to concentrate on the signs of Christ's presence and victory in the world we know. Since to be with God is heaven, and to be without God is hell, heaven and hell are earthly realities. The absolution in the new Anglican Communion rite prays, not that God will bring us to everlasting life, but that he will keep us in eternal life. The best evidence for heaven hereafter is provided by those experiences which seem to us both intensely good in themselves and to point beyond themselves. For some these experiences occur in an explicitly religious context, in communion or in contemplative prayer; for others, they occur, if at all, entirely outside the supposedly religious sphere. This does not make them any the less messengers from God since in so far as they are valid they point to a perfection and eternity only God can give.

68

The world contains a great deal that is beautiful, and the beauty is something "given". It is objective, even though it has to be subjectively apprehended. It is true that much of the beauty we experience is man-made, but here, too, there is an element of "givenness". Great artists, in words or sounds or pictures, are not inventors; they themselves respond to a vision and try to transmit it to others, aware always of their imperfect success. Art points beyond itself, to something in the world or beyond the world; and the world, when it moves us to tears by its beauty, points beyond itself. The beautiful in human life and relationships — moments of ecstasy, acts of love or heroism — these, too, are both real and enough in themselves to make life worth living, and at the same time give substance to hopes and longings that life on earth fails to satisfy completely. For one who does not believe in the resurrection, the best experiences of human existence do not, of course, lose their value but must remain in the last resort not only inexplicable but tinged with sadness, because they are so transitory. For one who is persuaded that life does not end with death, these experiences gain in solidity and worth, because they are not destined to be left behind, but taken up into a new life in which nothing is wasted. We shall take with us all that we have learnt, all that we have become. We shall share it with others in a perfect community, and we shall meet God, who in love set us here and in love drew us to himself. That, surely makes it all worth while.

NOTES

Chapter 1

1. Dietrich Bonhoeffer, *Letters and Papers from Prison* ed. Eberhard Bethge, tr. Reginald Fuller (S.C.M. Press 1967), p. 179.

2. Quoted in *Theology* (December 1967).

3. J.B. Phillips, *Making Men Whole* (Collins Fontana 1955), p. 92.

4. R.H. Benson, *Followers of the Lamb* (Longmans, Green 1905), p. 173.

5. Robert Short, *The Gospel According to Peanuts* (Collins Fontana 1966), p. 83.

6. Bernard Basset, *The Noonday Devil* (Burns & Oates 1964), p. 16.

7. Editorial in *Contact* (October 1966) — "The Waiting Room for Death."

8. C.V. Wedgwood, "Personality in History" III, in *The Listener* (20 March 1952).

9. See Charles Reid, *Malcolm Sargent* (Hamish Hamilton 1968), ch. 1.

Chapter 2

1. George Appleton, *On The Eightfold Path* (S.C.M. Press 1966), p. 48.

2. Tolstoy, *War and Peace* (Heron Books, London) vol. II, pp. 134-5.

3. Kathleen Raine, *Collected Poems* (Hamish Hamilton 1956), p. 159; cf. p. 140.

4. Valerie Pitt, *The Writer and the Modern World* (S.P.C.K. 1966), p. 79.

5. Laurence Whistler, *The Initials in the Heart* (Hart-Davis 1964), pp. 51-2.

6. Kathleen Raine, *Collected Poems*, p. 32; cf. p. 84.

7. Oscar Wilde, *The Ballad of Reading Gaol*.

8. Graham Greene, *The Heart of the Matter* (Penguin 1962), p. 210.

9. Quoted in N. Zernov, *Three Russian Prophets* (S.C.M. Press 1944), p. 136.

10. A.N. Whitehead, *Adventures of Ideas* (C.U.P. 1947), p. 213.

11. A.N. Whitehead, *Religion in the Making* (C.U.P. 1927), p. 138.

12. John Hick, "Theology and Verification" in *The Existence of God* (Macmillan, N.Y. 1964), pp. 260-1.

13. John Donne, *Sermons on the Psalms and the Gospels,* ed. Helen M. Simpson (University of California Press 1963), p. 211.

14. Kazoh Kitamori, *Theology of the Pain of God* (E.T. from 5th Japanese edn (1958) by M.G. Bratcher (S.C.M. Press 1965)), p. 19.

15. David Jenkins, *The Glory of Man* (S.C.M. Press 1967), p. 107.

16. Ibid, p. 110.

Chapter 3

1. *Interpreting the Resurrection* (S.C.M. Press 1967), p. 84.

2. Professor Roger Garaudy, as reported in *Frontier* (Autumn 1967), p. 222.

3. Paul Tillich, "Born in a Grave" in *The Shaking of the Foundations* (Pelican 1962), pp. 166-7.

4. Stuart Jackman, *The Davidson Affair* (Faber & Faber 1966), p. 113.

5. Dietrich Bonhoeffer, *Christology* (E.T., Collins 1966), pp. 44-5.

71

6. A.N. Whitehead, *Adventures of Ideas,* p. 275.

7. M.E. Glasswell, "The Use of Miracles in the Marcan Gospel" in *Miracles,* ed. C.F.D. Moule (Mowbray 1965), p. 162.

8. David Jenkins, op. cit., p. 34.

9. James McLeman, *Resurrection Then and Now* (Hodder & Stoughton 1965), p. 244.

10. David Jenkins, op. cit., p. 115.

11. J.E. Fison, *The Christian Hope* (Longmans, Green 1954), p. 194.

Chapter 4

1. Quoted in Robert Speaight, *Teilhard de Chardin* (Collins 1967), p. 209.

2. For a fuller discussion of this, see W.G. Pollard, *Chance and Providence* (Scribner's, New York, 1958).

3. P.B. Medawar, "Scientific Method" in *The Listener* (12 October 1967).

4. F.D. Maurice, *The Gospel of St John* (Macmillan 1885), pp. 66-7.

5. Teilhard de Chardin, *The Phenomenon of Man* (E.T., Collins Fontana 1965), p. 299.

6. A.J. Toynbee, *Hellenism* (O.U.P. 1959), pp. 45-6.

7. Paul Singleton, C.R., a paper read at St Albans in September 1965.

8. David Jenkins, op. cit., p. 117.

9. Fred Hoyle, "Man's Place in the Universe" in *The Listener* (9 March 1950).

10. William Jones, "An Essay on the Church" (1795), quoted by George Tavard, *The Quest for Catholicity* (Burns & Oates 1963), p. 128.

11. Rosemary Sutcliff, *Sword at Sunset* (Hodder & Stoughton 1963), pp. 189-90.

12. J.M. Neale, "Christ is Gone Up", *English Hymnal*, No. 166.

13. Kathleen Raine, "The Holy Shroud" in *Collected Poems* (Hamish Hamilton 1966), p. 151.

14. Christopher Wordsworth, "See the Conqueror Mounts in Triumph", *English Hymnal*, No. 145. Bishop Wordsworth also wrote the Easter hymn from which the titles of this and the preceding Chapter were taken.

15. Nicetas of Remesiana, *de Symbolo*, 10 (as quoted in J. Stevenson, *Creeds, Councils and Controversies* (S.P.C.K. 1966), No. 87, pp. 119-20.

16. F.D. Maurice, op. cit.

17. Thomas R. Kelly, *A Testament of Devotion* (Friends Home Service Committee 1949), p. 65.

18. John Betjeman, "House of Rest" in *A Few Late Chrysanthemums* 1954 — *Collected Poems* (2nd edn, John Murray 1962), p. 201.

INDEX

Adam	10, 12, 30
Agnostics	8, 27, 34
Anselm	13
Ascension, the	40, 62
Atheists	8, 34
Augustus	24
Auschwitz	13
Baptism	59, 60, 63, 66
Belsen	13
Benson, R.M.	4
Betjeman, John	68
Biblical quotations:	
Exod. 33. 23	45
Isa. 49. 15–16	21, 24
Matt. 7. 12	18
Matt. 28. 20	62
Mark 15. 34	7, 30
Luke 24. 39	44
John 19. 29. 30	30
Acts 26. 23	58
Rom. 6. 3–4, 11	60
1 Cor. 5. 19	26
1 Cor. 12. 13	60
1 Cor. 15. 8	33, 40

Eph. 1. 22; 5. 23   63

Phil. 3. 20   65

Col. 1. 18   63

Col. 1. 20   64

Col. 3. 1   58

Col. 3. 5, 11   59

Heb. 11. 14   65

1 Pet. 2. 11   65

Bonhoeffer, Dietrich   2, 3, 35

Browning, Elizabeth Barrett   15

Buddha, the   15, 19, 31, 55

Bultmann, Rudolf   34, 35

Bunyan, John   54

Canterbury, Archbishop of   36

Cartesianism   9

Christ   3, 4, 21, 23, 24, 25, 26, 27, 28,
                                29, 33, 35, 37, 38, 41, 42, 46,
                                50, 51, 57, 62, 66, 68

Christianity   9, 12, 20, 23, 24, 27, 28, 31, 34,
                                36, 42, 43, 44, 49, 51, 55, 58,
                                61, 63, 65

Church, the   2, 20, 38, 55, 56, 57, 58, 59, 62,
                                63, 64, 67

Clark, Neville   28

Communion of Saints, the   51, 53-4, 63, 64, 66, 67

Conversion   59, 61, 64

Cross, the   4, 24, 25, 26, 27, 28, 29, 30, 31,
                                34

Dante	9
Davidson Affair, The	33
Death	1, 3, 4, 5, 6, 7, 14, 15, 16, 17, 18, 32, 33, 43, 44, 45, 51, 53, 57, 64, 65, 66, 67, 68, 69
Demythologizing	11, 34
Departed, Prayer for	67
Desacralization	54, 55
Descartes	9
Devil, the	8, 10, 30
Donne, John	24
Dualism	8–10, 12
Edwards, Jonathan	2
Emmaus	41, 45
Empty tomb, the	36, 37, 38
Eve	10
Evil	9, 20, 25, 30
Evolution	11, 50, 51, 55, 57, 65
Faith	42, 45
Fall, the	8, 10–12, 13, 16, 18, 20
Fison, J.E.	46
Fitzherbert, Joan	41
Flecker, James Elroy	18
Freud	13
Furse, Jill	18
Garaudy, Roger	3, 30

Glasswell, M.E.	42
God	1, 2, 3, 8, 9, 10, 12, 13, 14, 17, 19, 20, 21, 22, 25, 26, 27, 28, 29, 30, 31, 32, 33, 42, 45, 47, 49, 50, 51, 53, 55, 59, 60, 64, 65, 66, 68, 69.
Gray, Thomas	14
Greene, Graham	19
Hamlet	5
Heaven	1, 19–20, 68
Hell	1, 16, 68
Hick, John	11, 20, 44
Hiroshima	3, 13–14, 24
Hooke, S.H.	41
Hoyle, Fred	57
Incarnation, the	23–4, 25, 39
Irenaeus	11, 12, 20
Jenkins, David	26, 42–3, 46, 56
Jesus *see* Christ	
John the Baptist	4
John the Evangelist	30, 37, 38, 50, 60, 63, 64
King Lear	16
Kitamori, Kazoh	26
Lampe, Geoffrey	36, 38, 39, 40, 41, 42
Laplace	3

Lazarus	38
Ling, Tevor	46
Love	17, 18, 19, 20, 22, 24, 26, 27
Luke, St	37, 62, 63
Mackinnon, Donald	39
McLeman, James	37, 42, 44
Mark, St	30, 37, 42
Marriage	7, 18
Marx, Karl	13
Matthew, St	30, 37, 62
Maurice, F.D.	2, 25, 50, 64
Medawar, Sir Peter	49, 51
Messiah, the	32, 33
Milton, John	10
Miracle	42, 50
Mohammed	56
Morison, Frank	28
Moses	44–5
Myers, Frederic	43
Mythology	9, 11, 15, 31, 36, 51
Niebuhr, R.	4
Noyes, Alfred	46
Objective immortality	34
Oedipus Rex	16
Original Sin	2, 12, 13
Orthodox Church, the	35, 46, 67

Paoli, General   5

Parousia, the   46

Patripassianism   26

Paul, St   6, 33, 38, 39, 40, 53, 58, 59, 60
61, 62, 66

Pelagianism   4

Phillips, J.B.   3—4, 13

Pitt, Valerie   16, 17

Platonism   9, 20

Pluralism   55

Preaching   35

Psychical research   43—4

Purgatory   1, 16

Raine, Kathleen   15—16, 18, 62

Raleigh, Sir Walter   1

Redemption, the   16, 17, 36

Resurrection   7, 33, 39, 43, 48, 51, 53, 58, 61,
63, 64, 66, 68, 69;

    of Christ   27, 28, 31, 33, 34, 35, 36, 40,
42, 43, 44, 45, 48, 51, 53, 57,
58, 62, 63, 67

Revivalism   2, 4

Sacraments   35, 42, 45, 46, 63, 66, 67

"Salvation history"   35—6

Sargent, Sir Malcolm   7

Schweitzer, Albert   27, 35

Science   48, 49, 54, 55

Shaw, George Bernard   33—4

Sin	4;
see also Original Sin	
Singleton, Fr Paul, C.R.	56
Socrates	6
Soloviev, V.	19
Soul, the	7, 53
Spirit, the Holy	60, 63
Spiritualism	43
Survival	6
Sutcliffe, Rosemary	61
Teilhard de Chardin, Pierre	48, 50, 51, 57
Thomas, Dylan	6
Thou Art There Also	1, 16
Tillich, Paul	32
Tolstoy	15
Total Depravity	13–14, 15
Traherne, Thomas	19
Trinity, the	26, 31, 56–7, 60, 63
Verification, Eschatological	23, 44
Wedgwood, C.V.	5
Wesley, John	2
Whistler, Laurence	18
Whitehead, A.N.	10, 12, 20, 34, 41, 55
Wilde, Oscar	19
Williams, Charles	19
Wootton, Lady	2

Yeats, W.B.   34
York, Archbishop of   7

Zoroaster   8